Advance praise for *Trust God, Love People*

"Reading this warm, charming story feels like sitting down with a close friend and sharing stories of faith and family—and the fiery courage that comes from deep conviction and perseverance."
—KIMBERLY SCHLAPMAN, founding member of the Grammy Award-winning country music band Little Big Town and author of *Oh Gussie!* and *A Dolly for Christmas*

"Jenny Marrs writes with a tender, open-hearted honesty that makes you feel less alone in your own longings and fears, a reminder that grace and goodness are always waiting on the other side of uncertainty."
—ERIN NAPIER, co-host of HGTV's *Home Town* and author of *Heirloom Rooms*

"Jenny's life is a testament to trusting in God's faithfulness, and her love for Jesus and people soaks through every story and every page. Her words are a balm to the soul."
—KORIE ROBERTSON, *Duck Dynasty* star and bestselling author of *The Duck Commander Family*

"Jenny believes that extraordinary, life-altering events are most often disguised as ordinary moments. Here, Jenny shares some of the ordinary moments that have brought her to extraordinary places. With warmth, wit, and authenticity, she tells her story as if you were sitting across from her at a café with a cup of coffee, losing track of time."
—MARIAN PARSONS, author of *Feels Like Home* and the blog Miss Mustard Seed

"*Trust God, Love People* is more than just Jenny's moving, heartfelt story; it's an inspiring blueprint for anyone wanting to build a life of spacious love and abundant joy. Opening this book is opening the door to the kind of really beautiful life of large love you've always imagined!"
—ANN VOSKAMP, *New York Times* bestselling author of *One Thousand Gifts*, *WayMaker*, and *Loved to Life*

"One of the most important theological disciplines, and yet often the most easily neglected, is a theology of remembrance. Jenny brings us back to this foundational aspect of the Christian life with remarkable honesty, theological clarity, and practicality. This will be a source of hope and courage for many."
—JOEL MUDDAMALLE, PhD, director of theology and research at Proverbs 31 Ministries and author of *The Hidden Peace*

"This book challenges the kind of life and love you think you can have and expands your vision for God's faithfulness in the ordinary and in-between days. Jenny calls us into a deeper trust and a fuller love with stories full of grace, grit, and redemption."

—CARLOS WHITTAKER, author of *Reconnected*

"Jenny points to God's unwavering presence in each and every moment. You'll laugh. You'll cry. And you'll fall deeply in love with this beautiful testimony. I am a firm believer that lives are changed and the enemy is defeated if we are courageous enough to share our testimonies, reminding us all that if He has done it for one, He can do it for you, too! This book is a blessing and inspiration to all!"

—HANNAH MOONEY, podcast host of *Unexpected with Hannah Love*

"I couldn't put this book down! I felt like I was sitting across from Jenny at a coffee shop, and she was sharing her testimony of God's faithfulness in good times and in trials. The authenticity on every page is so disarming. I could not recommend this book more!"

—LEANNA CRAWFORD, singer-songwriter

"This book is a beautiful, honest testimony to a pilgrim's faithful progress. It's also a radiant love story—love for God, love of family, love for ordinary miracles and extraordinary graces."

—JEFF CHU, author of *Good Soil* and *Does Jesus Really Love Me?*

"Jenny lives life with the front door wide open—to kids, llamas, TV crews, the unexpected, the hard, and the holy. This book is an irresistible invitation to step inside and be changed by her choice to welcome the world in."

—LISA-JO BAKER, bestselling author of *Never Unfriended* and *It Wasn't Roaring, It Was Weeping*

"Jenny offers us gentle wisdom and the sweetest reminders of God's love for us and our purpose in this life. Her heart is a gift, her way with words is a soothing balm, and *Trust God, Love People* is a treasure: a beautiful book by a beautiful soul."

—AMY HANNON, bestselling author, speaker, gatherer

TRUST GOD,

LOVE PEOPLE

TRUST GOD, LOVE PEOPLE

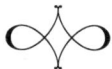

Stories of My
Openhanded Faith

JENNY MARRS

CONVERGENT

New York

Convergent
An imprint of Random House
A division of Penguin Random House LLC
1745 Broadway, New York, NY 10019
convergentbooks.com
penguinrandomhouse.com

Hardcover ISBN 978-0-593-44435-1
Ebook ISBN 978-0-593-44436-8

Printed in the United States of America on acid-free paper

1st Printing

First Edition

BOOK TEAM: Production editor: Loren Noveck • Managing editor: Allie Fox • Production manager: Sarah Feightner • Proofreaders: Cyrus Chin, Barbara Jatkola, and Caryl Weintraub

Book design by Debbie Glasserman

The authorized representative in the EU for product safety and compliance is Penguin Random House Ireland, Morrison Chambers, 32 Nassau Street, Dublin D02 YH68, Ireland. https://eu-contact.penguin.ie.

For my loves—

Dave, Ben, Nathan, Sylvie, Charlotte, and Luke

But don't be afraid of them! Just *remember* what the Lord your God did to Pharaoh and to all the land of Egypt. *Remember* the great terrors the Lord your God sent against them. You saw it with your own eyes! And *remember* the miraculous signs and wonders, and the strong hand and powerful arm with which he brought you out of Egypt.

DEUTERONOMY 7:18-19, NLT (EMPHASIS ADDED)

CONTENTS

CALLED TO TRUST

A few summers ago, my husband, Dave, and I cashed in airline miles and traveled with our five kids to the countryside of England. Despite it being early July, the air there was brisk. Mornings found me in front of a fire roaring inside a deep stone alcove, sipping steaming coffee and recording my thoughts in my worn leather travel journal. I had long dreamed of visiting the Cotswolds: The rolling hills covered in brilliant green grass and dotted with grazing sheep seemed the epitome of tranquility. The tree-lined country roads and the seemingly haphazard gardens full of brilliant roses, hydrangeas, and wild-flowers created settings for a beautiful painting. The beauty and natural expressions of our good God exceeded every expectation I had set before we arrived. The actual place was even more quaint and delightful than I had imagined.

The rambling ancient stone cottages with thatched roofs appeared straight from a fairy tale. I instantly fell in love with the muted colors of shutters and doors, the ivy-covered walls, and the steeply pitched roofs and prominent chimneys that exemplify "storybook-style" architecture. My design style and affinity for this aesthetic feel intrinsically linked to this place. It's as though my soul knew I would love it here before I ever stepped foot on the soil. Our family stayed in a charming cottage converted from a chapel in a small village, aptly named The Chapel. I adore the fact that in this part of the British countryside, the homes each have a name. Walking along this little stretch of road, you'll see The House on the Corner, The Old Cottage, Meadow House, and The New Inn. Homes here aren't just numbers lined down rows; they have names, identities. They are cherished.

We easily settled into village life. Slow mornings were spent reading and playing tag in the garden, followed by afternoon explorations of neighboring villages. We drank tea and slathered scones with decadent clotted cream and jam. In the evenings, after dinner at our local pub, we walked to the neighborhood playground, the sound of laughter floating through the air as the kids ran around the open field and climbed on the play structure. We laughed at ourselves as we attempted to emulate the lyrical accents of this lovely countryside. My daughter Charlotte started calling me "Mum," and I responded with "Yes, love?" or "Darling" (pronounced as an exaggerated "daah-ling").

One afternoon, we noticed a handwritten sign for fresh honey, and my son Ben and I walked over to purchase a jar. We hesitantly knocked on the front door of the neighboring cottage and waited for several minutes before we started to question whether anyone was home. Just as we turned to walk away, the kitchen window swung open, and an adorably plump character straight out of a movie greeted us. She was slightly taller than the windowsill, her face framed by silver curls and her rosy cheeks accentuated by a bright smile. She cheerfully sold us a large jar of honey, and I felt the urge to lean through the window and hug her. It was all too perfect to be real. We practically skipped home and immediately opened the jar to serve alongside the fresh cheese, bread, and pears we had picked up at the store on our way into town. I drizzled the rich golden liquid on a slice of cheese, and the aroma of warm sunshine and fragrant lavender filled the air. As we feasted on our brightly colored, abundant cheese platter out in the garden, I smiled contentedly and exhaled deeply.

While walking down the canopied path in front of The Chapel one morning, I bent low to pick up a single heart-shaped stone. I carefully jotted down the date on the rock with the marker I always carry when I travel. As I watched my five children walk carefree ahead of Dave and me, I slipped the stone into my bag, knowing it would be a tangible marker of God's faithfulness.

Standing on the cobblestone path of this quaint English village, I wanted to remember that on the other side of fear, there is great adventure and delight in store. Travel is a deeply vital part of my life, yet, for me, each trip is an intentional battle against fear. Stepping foot onto an airplane over the sea is an act of complete obedience and trust. Even if my knees are shaky and my heart is pounding, I know I can trust in God's faithful protection. Just like the little stone cottage with a name where I penned these words, I can rest in the fact that He has called me by name, and I am His. That simple truth is more powerful than any fear.

In the book of Joshua, the Israelites were instructed to gather stones to serve as a memorial to the Lord. Every time they looked at the stones, they were to be reminded of all God had done on their behalf. Whenever our family travels or when something meaningful happens in our lives, we collect a rock to mark the occasion. Later, if I find myself unsure of how God can work in what seems to be an impossible situation, I pick up one of the stones. I feel the weight in my palm. I turn it over and remember where I was standing when I lifted this particular stone from the earth and chose to carry it home.

We now have a sizable collection of rocks with dates and locations jotted along their jagged edges in permanent marker. They line bookshelves in our home and fill vintage bowls on our coffee table. When we encounter trouble, doubt, or fear, we can look to our stones and remember. We can remember how faithful He has been. We can remember His goodness, grace, mercy, and protection. We can remember who He is.

Like the stones my family collects, this book is a marker of the faithfulness of God. Many of the stories cover a season of my life when I became intimately acquainted with waiting. I called that season *the in-between*—where I held on to an expectant Hope even when the wait seemed to stretch endlessly. God spoke clearly during that season and continually reminded me: *Do not fear. I am here. I hear your prayers, and I see your tears. I'm at work. I'm going to do something that will astound you.*

While many of these stories reflect the years I spent

waiting—waiting to feel at home in a new town, waiting to fill our home with children, waiting to bring our daughter Sylvie home, waiting for our nonprofit work to bear fruit, I believe the flip side of the wait is equally important to share. I find it so creative of God to place me in a job where my primary focus is on a word I deeply resonate with: restoration. Through our business, Marrs Developing, and our TV show, *Fixer to Fabulous*, Dave and I work with families daily to restore old homes in our small Arkansas town. In restoring these often dilapidated, forgotten structures, we create a home where a family can build a life and make memories within previously unused spaces. A house is simply four walls and a roof. Yet a home is much more. My job is to create a home, to breathe life into an empty shell. In many ways, my job is akin to God's work in my life. His breath has restored the hollow places within my soul.

What I've found by turning over the stones that tell the story of my life is that in every situation, God has been gently ushering me into a place of steadfast trust. I have walked through dark valleys, clinging to His hand; I have spent long nights tossing and turning, fear threatening to overwhelm; and, yet, He has been ever faithful. He has never forsaken me. All along, He has been teaching me that when I keep my eyes on Him and take what I may think of as even the smallest, most seemingly insignificant step of faith, He will bless my efforts. And, in turn, I can choose to pour out the abundant love I have received to the people in my path. I can love the ones around my kitchen table and the ones across the sea. Every person He has brought into my life has impacted me, and I can, in turn, impact them. I've come to live my life by the phrase "Trust God, love people."

As you read the stories God has written in my life, I pray that you will take the time to pause and look back at your own story and marvel at your own markers of His faithfulness. Where has God met you in the past? What has He done that has astounded you? If you find yourself in the middle of your own long, dark night of waiting, I hope these stories can encourage your weary heart. If despair creeps at the door, remember: Our God never authors pain. He is only good. He is always faithful. He can be trusted. You, too, can *trust God and love people*.

TRUST GOD,
LOVE PEOPLE

CHAPTER 1

SMALL BEGINNINGS

While the defroster worked to melt the thin layer of ice on my windshield, I gently settled my one-year-old puppy, Bailey, onto his makeshift bed in the back seat. The honking of a horn caught my attention, and I glanced up to see Dave perched in the driver's seat of the U-Haul, motioning for me to roll down my window. As I did so, he grinned and shouted, "See you in Arkansas!" before pulling forward. With my former apartment in the rearview mirror, I took a deep breath, placed my hands on the steering wheel, and drove off, following him westward.

If someone had told me at my college graduation that I would go on to build a life far from my hometown, accept a job that involved plenty of public scrutiny, and eventually settle on a farm with five children and countless animals, I would have laughed. Never would I have believed that this shy girl raised thirty minutes from the ocean would end up with cows as her neighbors in Arkansas.

For the first two decades of my life, my world consisted of a white colonial in a quiet cul-de-sac in central Florida. My mom's side of the family all lived nearby and spent their days together at our family business—a wholesale bakery my great-grandma founded in 1951. My dad's mom, Grandma Shirley, watched my siblings and me after school while our parents worked. I'd often come home to find her in our kitchen, humming contentedly while stirring a skillet of seasoned ground beef, sizzling in preparation for dinner. I'd stand beside her, and together, we'd scoop the meat onto freshly steamed rolls, creating "loose-meat sandwiches," a recipe adapted from her favorite deli during her time living in Sioux City, Iowa. I loved listening to the colorful stories of her childhood in Chicago and how she and my grandpa spontaneously moved to Orlando, following friends toward the allure of the Sunshine State. I can still hear her melodic voice asking about my day as we worked. If my day was long or particularly hard, she'd start singing and clasp my hand so we could dance together in the kitchen, ignoring the simmering pot on the stove. Her deep, hearty laugh would incite my own.

I never would have imagined leaving the comfort of my family and beginning a life 1,200 miles away. And yet, here I was, driving behind Dave in the U-Haul that carried the contents of my former apartment, headed toward an unknown future.

At the time, I was in my early twenties and simply following my heart. For two years, Dave and I had been dating long-distance, and we were eager to live in the same zip code. Just nine days earlier, on Christmas Day, we had been poolside at my parents' house in Florida, our upturned faces warmed by the sun as we contemplated our future. During that conversation, we decided to quit our corporate jobs and move to Arkansas. Dave had briefly lived in Bentonville a few years before and knew I would love the town's charm. He also knew that the area was growing, and it was the right time to pursue his dream of building homes with his brother and dad, who had recently moved to Arkansas from Colorado.

The decision to move seemed simple: I wanted to be in the same city as the man I loved. In my naivete, I wasn't yet prone to overcomplicate the decision to pursue happiness. If we had waited even a handful of years, I might have been wrought with worry and indecision, focusing on logistics and what could go wrong. Thankfully, the decision was clear: Make the move. Follow the boy. Trust.

As we crossed an expansive bridge winding through the Arkansas River Valley, I called my mom to let her know we were getting close to Bentonville and fill her in on the gorgeous scenery around me. The rolling Ozark Mountains stretched as far as the eye could see, a fast-moving river cut through the valley below the bridge, and sparkling water rushed over boulders and rock formations. The beauty of my new state enthralled me. The region reminded me of my childhood summer vacations in the Smoky Mountains of western North Carolina.

Suddenly I spotted a chicken limping across the busy interstate. Around me, cars were swerving and honking their horns. I quickly hit my brakes and screeched to a stop. Now behind me in the U-Haul, Dave veered to the shoulder as the traffic around us slowed to a near standstill. Everywhere, chickens ran in various directions. I was entirely too freaked out to see the humor in the situation: the literal chickens crossing the literal road. Instead, I shouted to my mom, "A CHICKEN! Wait! CHICKENS! There are CHICKENS!" Bailey's ears perked up, and he jumped onto my lap to look out the window, barking un-controllably, alerting me to the danger. As I inched for-ward, I could see that chicken carcasses covered the stretch of black-tarred road before me; my mom yelled in response, "TURN AROUND AND COME HOME RIGHT NOW!"

The conversation with my mom was interrupted by a phone call from Dave, who, knowing me well, was calling to explain—in a deliberately calm tone—that a chicken truck had flipped over ahead.

A chicken truck.

He may as well have been speaking in Mandarin. I couldn't wrap my brain around what this combination of words could possibly mean. Growing up in suburban Or-lando, I had once begged my mom to call 911 when we saw a deer that had been struck by a car. Farm life and growing food were entirely foreign to me. I didn't under-stand how or why a truck would be full of chickens. I had never considered where my nuggets had originated.

I soon learned that Northwest Arkansas is a signifi-cant player in the poultry industry. This truck had been transporting thousands of chickens to a processing facil-ity when it swerved off the road, landed on its side, and expelled the poor chickens onto the busy highway.

As I watched the confused chickens wandering all over, I broke into tears, imagining their excitement at escaping the packed confines of the truck, racing toward the sunlight and dreams of freedom, only to meet their bitter end on that open stretch of interstate. The long drive had left me alone with my thoughts, and this chicken massacre felt like a flashing warning sign. The spontaneous decision to quit my job, pack up everything, and move to a town I had never even visited suddenly felt crazy and irrational.

As traffic started to move again, I glanced in the rear-view mirror and saw Dave pull back onto the highway. I restarted my ignition, turned on the radio, and heard a local station playing Keith Urban's "Who Wouldn't Want to Be Me." Still on the phone, Dave laughed as we both started singing along.

I believe extraordinary, life-altering events are most often disguised as ordinary moments. Looking back on the first day of new-hire training for my first corporate job after college, I can see how it set the course for my future. No, it wasn't the career move that I had hemmed and hawed and stewed over for months that was re-markable. It was the person I met while waiting in that registration line.

Standing among hundreds of other newly graduated, bright-eyed Corporate America Rookies, I looked around to see if I recognized anyone. I didn't. I tried my best to appear confident, waiting for my plastic name tag and a three-prong folder containing the agenda for the week. Sweaty-palmed, I felt like the new kid carrying my lunch tray in the cafeteria, desperately scanning for an empty seat next to a merciful comrade.

Just when I felt my nerves couldn't take one more moment of wondering how on earth I would make it through an entire week of training, a kind voice behind me said hello. I turned to find the kind voice accompanied by equally kind eyes and a warm, gentle smile.

"Hi. I'm Dave Marrs. I just moved to Bentonville, Arkansas, to run the territory there. What about you?"

It was a simple introduction—a few ordinary words followed by an ordinary handshake—yet the energy in the room shifted. My shoulders relaxed, and I felt at ease. If I could be friends with someone as magnetic and capable as Dave Marrs, then maybe I could survive the week ahead.

At the time, I was living in Tampa; Dave had moved from his home state of Colorado for this new job in Bentonville. That first week, Dave and I became instant friends. Our corporate sales jobs required a lot of time on the road checking on the stores we managed within our territories, which led to phone calls several times a day. For a time, we made these calls under the guise of sharing work-related information. But, as the months passed, we started talking more often, and the calls extended from quick chats to longer talks about our childhoods or our hopes for the future. I fell into the habit of calling him as I crossed the Howard Frankland Bridge on my drive home. I would share the humdrum details of my day and describe the beauty outside my window as the slanting rays of the setting sun cast a luminous glow over the bay.

A little over a year later, Dave received a promotion and moved to Chicago. He convinced me to join him for a weekend since he didn't know anyone there and knew how much I loved the city. As I rounded the corner of the arrivals terminal and spotted Dave holding his adorable handwritten sign, I nervously hugged him. My brain swirled as we descended the staircase, walked to the parking garage, and climbed into his SUV. What was I doing here? Why had I accepted his invitation to visit? Throughout the flight, I had convinced myself it was simple: He wanted a friend to help him explore and get to know his new neighborhood. I kept telling myself this was nothing more than a friend visiting a friend, and I just needed to calm down and act natural. But it was hard to act natural when I also felt new, unsettling emotions threatening to rise to the surface. Did I want to be more than friends?

As we buckled our seat belts and discussed where to get lunch, Dave suddenly turned to me, placing a hand on either side of my face, and drew me toward him for our first kiss. In an instant, every doubt dissipated. I know it sounds overly dramatic or cliché, but the world felt like it had stopped spinning. And, from that moment on, it was he and I.

That weekend, we feasted on pan-seared saganaki and eggplant moussaka in Greektown. We sipped champagne before stepping onto the glass observation deck at the top of the Hancock building. We sat on an old blanket on the shore of Lake Michigan, nibbling on cheese and crusty bread, watching dog walkers and bikers make their way along the lake. We window-shopped on the Magnificent Mile and ate thick, piping-hot deep-dish pizza. As we made our way home from dinner on my last evening there, our cabdriver asked how our night was going. Dave's response took us both by surprise. "Pretty great. I'm in love with this girl!" To this day, we laugh at the fact that he first professed his love for me to a taxi driver in Chicago.

Because we had built a friendship and gotten to know each other without the usual complications of daily life, our conversations held an immense depth that would have otherwise been missing had we started dating when we first met. Our love was built on a solid founda-

tion of genuine care, and this new stage in our relationship was full of joy and laughter and pure giddiness. I felt
like the luckiest girl in the world to be holding my best
friend's hand and envisioning a future together.

Several months later, I was promoted and moved to
Nashville. Every Friday for the next year, we would drive
to meet halfway-ish in Louisville, Kentucky. There, we'd
park one car and drive together the rest of the way to
our respective cities. In Nashville, we'd spend long weekends hiking the trails on the outskirts of the city, eating
picnic lunches on the banks of breathtaking waterfalls.
In Chicago, we often walked a few blocks to the small
corner video store, taking our time perusing the latest
titles before eventually deciding on one. We'd stroll back
to his apartment, admiring the city's historic architecture. Inside, we'd turn on the radio, open a bottle of wine,
and cook dinner together in his tiny kitchen. We'd laugh
as we bumped elbows and danced around each other to
grab another pot or stir the sauce before it bubbled over.
Our plates balanced precariously on our laps as we ate
steaming pasta and watched our chosen movie.

The visit to the movie rental store was the start of an
entire date night. When we try to explain this concept to
our kids today, they bewilderedly stare at us as though
we are describing life before the invention of the light-
bulb. I think the fact that this experience can never be

re-created—thanks to the countless streaming services now available at our fingertips—makes it even more special.

That one simple handshake in an ordinary conference room all those years ago changed the trajectory of my life. At the time, I couldn't have known the cute boy standing before me was my future husband, father of my children, and business partner. I couldn't have known that we would go on grand adventures together and visit places I had only read and dreamed about since childhood. I couldn't have known that we would start a life together and eventually move to a farm where we would raise babies and animals and find deep contentment in quiet moments in an old house nestled in the shadow of the Ozark Mountains.

In the almost two decades following the fateful day when I was introduced to my new state with a chicken-truck massacre, I have learned of the faithfulness of God and the way He tenderly guides us one small step at a time. Had I known what adventures, pitfalls, victories, and hardships were ahead, I probably would have felt overwhelmed by the enormity of the tasks and found myself paralyzed in fear, unable to act. Or I might have turned the car around and headed right back to the comfort of familiarity in Florida.

Looking back at all I've walked through in my life, particularly since arriving in Northwest Arkansas, I can see how God protected me from knowing the full scope of what He had in store before I was ready. Thankfully, God tells us not to despise small beginnings, for He rejoices to see the work begin (Zechariah 4:10). He wants us to *begin* the work, to simply do the one small thing before us. To drive the car across the state line and trust Him as He leads. Even when a flock of chickens blocks our path, we need to keep on driving. Especially then. We need to trust even when the bigger picture is murky and unknown and the way ahead seems rife with obstacles and opposition.

On that cold day in January all those years ago, that's exactly what we did. We swerved around the chicken massacre and drove on, our eyes focused on the uncharted horizon before us.

CHAPTER 2

FINDING HOME

The day after we arrived in Bentonville, I hopped into the front seat of the U-Haul with Bailey in my lap as Dave drove us to visit a house that was for rent. It was a modest house, one most people would consider a fixer-upper, but to us, it was adorable and held nothing but potential. We took a quick tour with the landlord and immediately signed a lease. When he asked when we would like to move in, we gestured to the U-Haul in the driveway and answered, "How about now?"

Right away, we unlatched the roll-up truck door and

started unpacking. First out of the truck was my beloved red sofa, my celebratory purchase with my first "real" paycheck after college. I loved the sofa and all it represented: years of hard work in school, landing a job, and the pride of creating a home on my own. The sofa had moved with me from Florida to Tennessee and now to Arkansas. Next, we unloaded a hand-me-down wood kitchen table and chairs my parents had given us for our new home. Later, we painted the table white and the four chairs a bright and cheery red. We would go on to spend countless nights around that happy little table.

After making our way through dozens of boxes, we carefully unpacked the oversize black-and-white framed print of the Eiffel Tower I had bought while working at a home decor store in college. At the time, it was an extravagant purchase, but I justified buying the print because it was a representation of the magical city I dreamed of visiting one day. Dave had surprised me with plane tickets to Paris for Christmas, and now, with our tickets in hand, he ceremoniously hung my beloved print in a prominent position: right over our new-to-us fireplace.

During those first months in Bentonville, I was surprised by how much of an adjustment it was to go from living in a big city to a town with a population of less than thirty thousand people. I was instantly smitten with how charming and idyllic Bentonville was, yet I found myself uneasy with its subtle cultural nuances. Having grown up in a small town, Dave would chitchat with every stranger he met, while I felt a need to be on guard, diligent in my Stranger Danger upbringing. While Dave would casually talk about the weather with the person in front of us in the grocery store checkout line, I would smile and nod, subconsciously tightening my grip on my purse in case the innocent small talk was simply a diversion by this seemingly harmless granny who very well could have been a professional thief.

I also struggled to get used to the slower pace of small-town life, particularly on the road. I was accustomed to multilane freeways, and while I'm not proud of it, I received my fair share of speeding tickets in high school and college. The two-lane roads and Sunday drivers in Arkansas induced frustration. But even though I often felt like I was crawling along the road, the first time another driver waved to me as we passed each other, I was so delighted and caught off guard that I couldn't pull myself together quickly enough to respond with a return wave.

In that season, I felt unsettled, and yet I knew, deep down, that there was a purpose for this move. Even if there wasn't a sandy beach or palm tree in sight, and I often longed for old friends and familiar neighborhoods, I could sense God's hand had guided Dave and me here.

I just needed to trust that we were where we were supposed to be and give it time.

After our move, Dave and his brother and dad quickly got to work creating Marrs Construction, working around the clock to set up the corporation, finalize the general contractor licensing process, and secure loans to build their first round of homes. Dave found a house plan online, used the loans to buy an inexpensive lot in the neighboring town of Bella Vista, and broke ground on his first home thirty days after we arrived in Arkansas.

I, on the other hand, still needed to find a job. Dave often came home at midday to let me borrow "The Red Dragon"—a 1987 Chevy pickup truck he had bought from the classifieds in nearby Kansas City for $1,000—so that I could go to job interviews. We'd laugh as I climbed into the rusty old truck in my interview pantsuit and high heels.

I submitted dozens of résumés and went on countless interviews, yet I left each with the same lackluster outlook: I would never find a job I was passionate about. Dave encouraged me to wait for the right job to come along rather than settle for something that wouldn't make me happy in the long run. However, we both knew that we needed income, and we needed it soon.

When my birthday rolled around, twenty days after moving to town, I came home from another disheartening interview to find our home filled with Dave's family and the handful of friends we had in the area. I shrieked in surprise and joy to find our house full of people I loved. I firmly believe that filling a house to the brim with people and laughter makes it feel like a home, and this surprise party was exactly what I needed in that moment when I was feeling untethered in this new place. I gratefully accepted hugs and soaked in the cheerful energy. We ate pizza on paper plates and plugged in the karaoke machine after I had blown out the candles on my cake. I'll never forget Grandma Marrs and me linking arms and swaying together as we belted "Pour Some Sugar on Me" into the microphone. We danced and sang, and, once again, our new life in this new place felt hopeful and full of possibilities.

A month later, I accepted a job offer. I started working for a consumer packaged-goods company, managing products I actually liked (and Dave loved getting free samples). I made a handful of good friends, who are some of my closest friends to this day. I bought a car, fell into a daily routine, and began experimenting with painting walls and furniture to make our house feel like home.

Slowly, I found new rhythms and felt myself becoming more settled. I was adjusting to living in a winter climate for the first time and was initially charmed by the bitter cold and dreary days. Dave would light fires and I would snuggle under cozy blankets. I bought a cute new coat and learned to accessorize with scarves. But as the days turned to weeks, the barren trees, dead grass, and overcast skies lost their novelty and I found myself desperately missing the palm trees and balmy coastal breezes of home. I ached for the warmth of the sun and the beauty of a clear blue sky. I wondered if I could handle living in a place where I was forced to replace my staple footwear of flip-flops for closed-toe shoes for months on end.

Just when this Florida girl couldn't take another dismal and blustery day, I noticed the faintest hint of green returning to the trees. As the long nights of winter faded into the early days of spring, I was enthralled by the sheer beauty of the deep magenta redbud blooms, the brightly colored daffodils unfolding, and the intensely green grass. Seemingly overnight, I had stepped out from under a dreary haze into a vibrant, colorful world. I marveled at each bloom as though I were witnessing a miracle take place before my eyes. And, in a way, I was. I had never before experienced the absolute wonderment of spring. It felt as though the whole world were waking up from a long slumber, and I responded in earnest by throwing open the windows to let the refreshing breeze clear the stale air from our home. I began to see that the changing of the seasons represents the natural expression of new grace and fresh mercies. These beautiful reminders of how spring's bounty always returns after the desolate winter were everywhere.

With the change in weather, I started going for a run on a nearby trail after work each day. The trail loops around a small lake and meanders through a forest. As each breathtaking day of spring progressed, I was captivated by the colors and the scents along my running route. The leaves were practically neon, the green so vibrant it was almost unreal. The blush-colored blooms of dogwood trees created a magical, otherworldly experience.

As I finished up one of my evening runs, I reached into my pocket for my car key and realized it wasn't there. I retraced my path, knowing it must have fallen out somewhere along the trail. As I searched for the missing key, I began to panic. All the way back to the car, my mind raced with fears that a) my car had been stolen or b) a murderer was now hiding in its back seat.

The reality turned out to be beyond my imagination: Someone had found my key fob on the ground, hit the button to see which car beeped, and then set the key on the hood. No fanfare. No rifling through the purse sitting in plain sight on my seat—admittedly, my common sense was not up to the level of my worst-case-scenario imagination—no reward money expected, no hidden killer in my back seat. Just a kind gesture.

My mind reeled. Where am I living? Who are these people? They wave at me when I drive or walk by, they greet me with a hello and ask how I'm doing with such genuine sincerity that I believe they actually care about my answer, and they return my car key without so much as swiping the loose change from the cup holder.

That was the moment I knew that this was becoming home.

The beautiful thing about creating a home is that it can happen anywhere. And I had to learn that, just like building a house, building a home doesn't happen overnight. It takes time. In the early months (and years) here, I was often overwhelmed by all I needed to learn about this new place. I missed my friends and family back in Florida. There were days that I physically ached for the comfort of familiarity. Yet, each day, I settled in a little more. I found back-road shortcuts to the office. I found my favorite taco place and coffee shop. I hosted my parents and siblings for weekend visits and proudly showed off my new town. Dave and I spent Sunday afternoons exploring new trails and neighboring towns.

As we created memories here, I saw how God uses seasons of change to teach us about His character and faithfulness. By moving to a new town without a safety net or backup plan, I learned to place my trust in Him alone. I failed and misstepped often. Yet, as the years unfolded and I continued placing one foot in front of the other into the unknown, I graciously found God's plans continued to be infinitely higher and grander and better than anything I ever could have dreamed up on my own.

CHAPTER 3

WITHIN THE WALLS

As our big trip to France later that spring approached, I found myself jotting notes in the margins of my beloved travel books while I sat at red lights, or spending my lunch hour researching off-the-beaten-path places to visit. Dave would laugh as I practiced my mediocre French in the evenings. I whispered prayers of gratitude each morning as I reflected on how God had walked me through a season of change and uncertainty into one full of excitement and expectation. I was beginning to understand that when I allowed God to author my story, I could eagerly turn the page in anticipation of what was to come.

That May, I took a deep breath as Dave and I, along with his brother, Matt, and his sister-in-law, Karey, boarded a plane headed to Paris. It was my first flight over the Atlantic, and I was giddy to finally visit the City of Light. We landed and launched immediately into tourist mode, exploring picturesque side streets, devouring Nutella-and-banana crepes from sidewalk stands, and finding ourselves awestruck by the intense beauty of the city. We walked inside Notre-Dame cathedral and silently took in the enormity of the sacred space. The city lived up to every one of my high expectations and surpassed them tenfold. Walking the real-life streets under the soft amber glow of the ancient streetlamps was much better than anything I had read about in my stack of guidebooks.

On our third evening, we visited the top of the Eiffel Tower. The historic elevator was crowded, and after the doors opened, we were jostled along by the dense crowd onto the outer deck of the tower overlooking the city. Dave seemed anxious; as I found out later, the mass of tourists had dampened his romantic plans for a private moment. After we descended, Matt and Karey went off in search of gelato while Dave and I stayed behind. I wasn't ready to step out of the magic of the evening just yet. As we stood there, looking up at the glow of the sparkling lights against the clear, dark sky, Dave turned to me and said, "Marry me" in a voice mocking a popular commercial at the time. I laughed and said, "But of course!" To which he replied, "I'm serious." And then, in what can only be described as an out-of-body experience, I watched as he dropped to one knee and held up a small box containing an engagement ring.

Matt and Karey came running. They had heard my ecstatic shriek and knew he had proposed. We took photos and then went to find a café, where we popped champagne and admired my new ring. Until that point, I had forgotten to even look at it. I didn't care about the ring. I only cared that he had asked.

The next year passed in a beautiful blur of wedding planning. We traveled back and forth to Florida every couple of months to plan our wedding there. We toured a dozen reception sites before visiting a historic resort just outside of Orlando. It was surrounded by ancient oak trees, tranquil lakes, and rolling hills. The Mediterranean architecture, peaceful landscape, and timeless elegance won us over immediately.

One afternoon, just after returning from a visit to Florida to meet with caterers, Dave called me at work and asked if I'd meet him for lunch. I assumed we would review seating charts or one of my many checklists. Instead, he picked me up at the office and drove me to a vacant lot in a neighboring town to where we were renting. As I wondered what we were doing there, he unlocked the car door, walked around to my side, and opened the door for me. I accepted his extended hand and we walked together onto the tree-laden lot.

"It's ours," he stated matter-of-factly and smiled. He went on to explain that a realtor friend had called him about this lot. It wasn't yet on the market, but the friend knew Dave's desire to buy a lot in town to build a house for us. I looked at him incredulously.

"It's really ours?"

"It's really ours."

My eyes widened and a broad smile stretched across my face. I was shocked in the best possible way. That night, we scoured the internet for house plans. We eventually found one that fit our aesthetic, as well as the size of the lot. We worked for weeks modifying the original plan—moving a wall here, rotating the staircase there—before agreeing it was perfect. We broke ground not long after, with the goal of finishing the house before our wedding day.

I fell hard for the process of choosing paint colors and cabinet hardware and searching for unique lights. Dave and I laid out the bookshelves for the office he would build. His dad and brother helped him with the trim work and framing. Every afternoon, I'd leave the office and join Dave for lunch at the house while he worked on installing tile floors or welding handrails. At night, I dreamed of wedding dresses and kitchen cabinets. I couldn't have known then how the experience of designing and building this home would shape my future career, but looking back on how God was weaving these details into my story, I'm immensely grateful.

Just two months before our wedding, as the house was nearing completion, I made sure Dave was working on another jobsite before I snuck over to our newly drywalled home. As dusk approached, I lined the staircase with candles and created a makeshift picnic on our balcony. Atop a timeworn quilt, I set out a charcuterie board, a bottle of champagne, two glasses, and half a dozen candles. As the sky continued to shift toward nightfall, I lit each candle and waited for Dave to arrive.

When he opened the front door, he was greeted by the flickering glow of candlelight and the soft hum of music. We walked through the house, hand in hand, and dreamed of filling it with memories and laughter and, someday, babies. We sat on the blanket, nibbled on cheese, and toasted our future together.

Our wedding day was one of the windiest on record for early April in Florida, and my veil and hair twirled throughout the ceremony, as my childhood pastor married us outside. Grandma Shirley sang. Our eyes glistened with joyful tears. My dad painstakingly baked our stunning wedding cake, and because he knows of my deep affinity for cake, he made a miniature version as a gift for each of our 250 guests. We danced late into the night, surrounded by our family and lifelong friends. We celebrated the absolute wonderment of finding each other. We marveled at the fact that every person we loved most in the world was there, gathered in one room for one magical night. It was a day we would never, ever forget.

After our honeymoon, we moved into our new home, I went back to ordinary days at work, and Dave went back to building houses. Life was good. Yet I sensed something missing. I had loved planning and executing the details that went into making our wedding day special and our home ours. But now the wedding was over, our home was built, and all my creative juices were left spinning inside my head with nowhere to go.

Dave could see I was missing this creative outlet, and so he gifted me a DSLR camera. Photography uniquely unlocked my creative side. I loved feeling the weight of the camera in my hands. Learning about ISO and aperture felt like discovering a new world. I took photos of everything and everyone in my path. I loved capturing life from behind the lens. Eventually, friends started asking for photos of their families or special moments. I spent evenings and weekends snapping shots of my nieces and nephews. I photographed a friend's wedding. I still worked full-time, but this new hobby fulfilled me in a way that my corporate sales job couldn't.

The next spring, Dave saw an ad in the newspaper for an abandoned house for sale in our town's downtown district. We met there one afternoon during my lunch break, and as we walked through the 800-square-foot house, I kept saying, "It's perfect." Even though, by most rational standards, it was far from perfect. It was in terrible condition—rotten floors and walls yellowed from years of smoke damage. But at the time, houses in downtown Bentonville were selling for pennies on the dollar, and we knew this would be a smart investment. Right then and there, we decided we would renovate the house and turn it into my photography studio.

We were ecstatic about the project. It would be our first restoration. We stayed up late at night dreaming and planning, and we walked through the house dozens of times, waiting for the paperwork to close. Once the purchase was finalized, we spent that first weekend pulling up carpet and tile, then evenings after work removing trash and debris.

As the renovation continued, I fell hard for that little house. I could physically feel it come back to life as we worked to restore it. The previously sad, heavily laden house became a bright and cheerful cottage over the course of many months of work. We painted the exterior a rich blue and filled the front porch with plants and flowers. I placed a potted lemon tree in the corner of the living room, where the southern sun's rays bathed it each morning. When the house was ready, I set up a small studio in one bedroom and an office in the other. I took photos of newborns in that studio and often sat at the kitchen table instead of in the office to edit photos so that I could open the back door to let in the breeze and listen to the lyrical melody of birds in the yard. My nana came to visit and stayed in that house, declaring it to be a perfect little home. I agreed.

During the renovation, as we were removing the rickety kitchen cabinets, Dave used a sledgehammer to knock through the wall separating the kitchen from the living room. Sheetrock exploded from the impact, then he stopped short of the second blow and shouted for me to take a look. I peered into the hole to see that there, hidden behind the drywall, was a stack of papers that had yellowed over time. Dave gently lifted them out, and we were surprised to find they were handwritten letters.

The slanted handwriting described life overseas during the Second World War. They had been written to a love waiting back home. We sat on the dusty, Sheetrock-covered kitchen floor and read every word, moved to tears. This home had held words of love within its walls all these years. We donated the letters to our town's historical society, but the fact that they had been left there alone broke my heart.

Finding those letters was evidence of the way a home holds the stories of its previous owners within its walls. They were tangible proof of a life lived under that roof before we ever stepped inside. Our job was to respect and honor those stories while paving the way for new ones to be written. Restoring that little cottage was pivotal for us. At the time, we just enjoyed the process and decided to restore another if the opportunity presented itself (it did, again and again). But more than that, I noticed and was grateful for all the ways God had shown Himself to be the faithful author of an incredible story in my life—from marrying my best friend to developing the creative gifts He'd given me to learning to honor the stories held within walls.

CHAPTER 4

JUST KEEP GOING

One sunny June afternoon, I became intimately acquainted with the dark cast of grief's shadow when I was blindsided by the hollowness of losing a life within my womb. We hadn't told anyone that we were trying to get pregnant, so Dave and I grieved together silently. Our new home that we had been so excited to build and move into transformed from a place of hopeful anticipation into four walls seeped in sorrow. I remember walking to a neighbor's house for dinner one evening and thinking, *How can we sit here and eat and act normal?* Nothing made sense.

One afternoon, I grudgingly pulled myself off the sofa, tied my shoes, and decided I would run again. The tempo of my feet hitting the pavement helped me to focus on something outside of my pain and heartache. At first, my heart pumped fast, and my breath came in short bursts. I focused on slowing it down; I took a deep breath in and counted to myself, "One, two, three," then I exhaled, "One, two." As my feet hit the pavement in sync with my breath, I felt stronger. I prayed as I ran. Tears pooled in my eyes. I wiped them and kept running, kept asking, "Why, Lord? Why?"

After that, I started running each day. At first, my lungs burned, and my weak leg muscles trembled from the strain. As the days stretched into weeks, my strength improved, and I started running longer stints without pausing to walk or stretch my tight muscles. I found new inner strength, as well. My heart slowly stitched itself back together as my legs pounded out mile after mile. Always, I prayed as I ran. As the weeks turned to months, I began to wonder if there could be a purpose to this season of loss and waiting to start our family. I didn't yet fully understand what that purpose might be—and I wouldn't for many, many years—but I could vaguely begin to see the faintest hint of light through the dense fog of despair.

I signed up to run the Healdsburg Wine Country Half Marathon later that year with my friend Casey. We determined if we were going to torture ourselves by running 13.1 miles, we would reward ourselves with good wine afterward.

My parents, along with my younger brother and sister, flew to California to meet me, Dave, Casey, and her husband, Matt. The night before the race, I stepped off a curb and onto the side of my foot rather than my heel. I rolled my ankle, and the pain radiated up my leg. I didn't cry. Instead, I laughed. "I'm still running this race," I declared.

And I did. The pain from my injured ankle dissipated around mile six. At mile eight, my dad drove a rented minivan alongside Casey and me as we ran. The side door was all the way open, and Dave, my brother, and Matt all hung out of it, wildly waving and cheering us along. My mom shouted from the passenger seat, and my sister stood through the open sunroof. I heard Dave's booming voice, "You've got this, babe! You're so close! Keep going!" My feet moved from a slow shuffle and picked back up into a well-paced stride. The van could only go so far on the route. Dave shouted, "We'll see you at mile ten!"

As I rounded the bend at mile marker ten, I saw everyone waving enthusiastically and cheering loudly. I chuckled and felt buoyed to pick up my pace once again. Casey and I had separated earlier, but I couldn't slow down; I was so close to the finish line. I kept going. I focused on keeping my breath in rhythm with my feet hitting the pavement. At mile twelve, the pain in my ankle was excruciating. I didn't think I could make it another mile. As I crested the final hill of the course, the sight of the golden rays of sunrise hitting the vineyard took my breath away. Even as I tried to concentrate on the beauty before me, I was furious with my body. This wasn't a new sensation—I had grown very accustomed to being furious with my body for not being able to do what I wanted it to do. I felt the pinprick of tears as my frustration mounted.

I slowed my pace to a walk. I was defeated.

"Let's go! You are not quitting. You've worked too hard. You're so close!" Dave shouted as he left the crowd at the sidelines and came to join me on the racecourse. I hadn't seen him in the crowd because I was staring straight forward, willing myself to go on. As he ran toward me, my whole body ached, but I forced my feet to move. We paced together for 1.1 miles. He wasn't wearing running shoes, and his jeans couldn't have been comfortable to run in. Still, his encouragement sustained me, and we crossed the finish line—together.

"Thank you. I couldn't have made it without you," I said, once I was able to speak.

"You are stronger than you think, Jenny Marrs," he responded resolutely.

The next day, we toasted to accomplishing something I hadn't thought I was physically capable of doing. When we arrived back home, I hung the race bib on the wall as a reminder: Hard things are hard. We simply must keep putting one foot in front of the other to get through them.

At the time, Dave and I didn't know that the next decade would be fraught with hard things. But we learned something at mile marker twelve in the middle of a vineyard in Northern California: Together, we can do hard things, especially with the cheers from our loved ones on the sidelines sustaining us. And, always, the hard things will be balanced with goodness and beauty. Like the view on the final hill of the course as the amber-colored vineyards caught the sunlight in a display of autumnal majesty. Despite the pain, the beauty remained.

Two years later, I walked in the door, sweaty from a long run, and heard my phone ring. My sister-in-law was calling to share happy news: She was pregnant, and I would become the proud aunt to another niece. She now knew Dave and I had been trying to start a family, and I could hear the hesitancy in her voice as she gently shared the good news. I eagerly congratulated her, and we chatted for a few minutes about how she was feeling and how excited I was for her and my brother-in-law. I appreciated how careful she was to share it with me privately, but I was upset with myself for putting her in that position. She knew I would struggle to separate her joy from my pain.

After we said our goodbyes, something broke inside me. The self-protecting dam that I had spent the last couple of years carefully constructing burst wide open, and my tears gushed forth in a torrent. My knees gave way, my body sinking to the floor as my vision tunneled, and my breath came in jagged waves between deep, guttural sobs.

I heard the faint click of the door unlatching as Dave returned home. "Oh, babe," he whispered as he turned to find me huddled on the kitchen floor, enveloped in sorrow. His brother had already called him with their news and Dave rushed home to check on me. He cupped my face in his calloused hands, wiping the streaks of mascara-stained tears from my cheeks, then looped his arm beneath mine and helped me to stand.

"It's okay. It's going to be okay," he reassured me as we

slowly made our way out of the kitchen and into our bedroom. My frail frame leaned against his strong one as he helped me into our bed, where I lay down and closed my eyes. I felt hollow and tired. Dave stepped into the bathroom, and I heard the sound of the tap turning on.

By that time, the longing we had to start a family had reached a fever-pitch level of desperation. My entire world revolved around sheer frustration with my body for not being able to do the one thing it was naturally supposed to do: create life.

Each month began with a small glimmer of hope and ended with a brutal puncture to that fragile bubble. I had started seeing doctors and fertility specialists, and was constantly being poked and prodded. As I sat at my doctor's office waiting for my name to be called for more blood work or another test or procedure, I'd solemnly look around at the glowing faces and swollen abdomens of these other women whose bodies had clearly gotten the memo.

Most nights, I awoke from a recurring nightmare. In it, the doctor placed a tightly swaddled newborn babe into my expectant arms. When I looked down to see their eyes and soak in their tiny, perfect nose, the baby was gone. My arms were empty. The warmth from the body still radiated onto my forearms and against my chest, but the weight was gone. I screamed in terror and woke up panting, gasping for breath. My chest ached. I reached for my inhaler and breathed in the medicine, visualizing it opening my lungs and pouring life back inside.

In our room, Dave tenderly said, "I ran a bath for you." Slowly, I stepped into the warm water and let the lavender scent of the bath salts envelop me. I heard him leave the room as I lay there with my eyes closed, taking deep breaths. He returned with an armful of candles and lit each one. He set two on the counter and then three on the window ledge above the bathtub before he turned off the light and walked over to where I lay, soaking and breathing.

"I love you. And I don't know how, but I know we will get through this. It's going to be okay. Somehow, it will be," he whispered as he leaned over and kissed me gently on the forehead. The lesson carried home from that vineyard in California came to mind: Together, we can do hard things.

I sat in the tub, my sorrow swirling in that dark water. The steam rose, and with it I could feel a sense of peace and a small sliver of hope rising within me. I closed my eyes and whispered the only prayer I could muster at that moment. "Please, Jesus. Please." I sensed the gentle words, *Your story isn't over yet.*

That night, I slept soundly.

CHAPTER 5

DOUBLE PORTION

Dave and I took the familiar thirty-minute drive to my doctor's office to learn about a new procedure that gave me an estimated fifty percent chance of becoming pregnant. We sat in her office and listened to her outline what the next four weeks would entail. As we listened, Dave firmly held my hand as I held back tears. He knew how desperately I wanted this to work, how deeply I wanted someone to rekindle my smoldering embers of hope, but I was afraid. I was dreading the prescriptions, the doctor visits, the blood draws, the hospital stays, and, most of all, I was afraid it wouldn't work, and my heart would shatter for good this time.

Twelve days after the final procedure, I woke early and drove to the clinic alone before work to have my blood drawn. This would tell me whether or not I was pregnant. On the way, I talked to God. I told him that I knew He wanted me to be a mother; there was simply no other explanation for this fierce desire planted in my soul. I also explained to Him that I needed His strength today. During that quiet drive, I felt an assuring and calm presence in the car with me. As tears pooled in my eyes, I felt a profound sense of peace. I distinctly heard God whisper, *I am with you.* I knew that, regardless of the outcome, I could trust Him.

That afternoon, after an excruciating day of waiting, I shouted for Dave when the familiar number appeared on my phone's screen. My voice trembled as I answered. After exchanging pleasantries, I held my breath as the nurse spoke. I heard nothing after the three words I'd waited years to hear: "Congratulations, you're pregnant!" A laugh of exuberant joy escaped my lips as Dave scooped me up and twirled me around in his arms.

Due to my high hormone levels, the doctor believed it was likely I was carrying multiples; at my first sonogram, the sonographer pointed out the two distinct gestational sacs on the screen, and I squealed. Dave and I looked at each other, beaming. It was too good to be true. After heartache and grief, we had been given beauty for ashes and now celebrated a double portion of joy (Isaiah 61:3-7).

A month later, I wrapped framed ultrasound photos and gifted them to Dave's and my parents, our siblings, and our three grandmothers for Christmas. The room filled with jubilant shrieks and laughter as they unwrapped the frames. My sisters both cried, and my mom held me as tears fell down our cheeks. My sister-in-law and I celebrated that we were expecting cousins who would grow up together. My dad waited quietly, holding the photo and wiping away tears. When my mom let go, he enveloped me in a tight embrace.

After so many years of longing for children, I treasured every single moment of pregnancy. I was one of those obnoxious pregnant women who truly loved the way my body morphed as the weeks turned into months. I was giddy shopping for maternity clothes and diligently took photos in front of a chalkboard every week to document the growth of my expanding belly. Thankfully, I never suffered from morning sickness. Just the opposite: I had increased energy and felt my absolute best. My eyes shone, and my cheeks glowed. Each evening, I'd read my What to Expect pregnancy book and explain to Dave that the babies were the size of an avocado or a mango. I walked every evening after work and went to Pilates several times a week. I happily cut deli meats and unpasteurized cheeses from my diet. (Granted, I added dozens of Grandma Marrs's peanut butter cookies into my diet to balance out the restrictions.)

On February 23, 2010, the ultrasound wand rolled over my swollen abdomen and revealed two healthy little boys kicking each other. Dave and I burst into joyful laughter. Boys! We had already created a short list of baby names, and the moment we left the clinic, we narrowed it down to the top four boy names. I had been reading a book with a little brown-haired boy named Ben as the main character. As soon as I read the name, it went to the top of my list. Dave agreed, and we had already decided on his middle name, William, after my beloved grandpa. My papa was kind, generous, brave, and had the most contagious laugh imaginable. He fought a long, hard battle with ALS and MS and had passed away when I was fourteen. Throughout his fight, his smile, faith, and courageous spirit remained steadfast. To this day, he is my hero. I was elated to no longer refer to "Baby A" but instead use his name: Benjamin William Marrs.

We took a family vote for Baby B: Our short list included Nathan, Evan, and Ethan. After the vote, Nathan was the overwhelming winner. His first name would pair perfectly with the middle name we had chosen,

Kean (pronounced Kane), which was Grandma Marrs's maiden name. Grandma Marrs was ninety-one years old and the most gregarious, spunky, and energetic person I knew. From the first moment I met her, she accepted me into the family fold with enthusiasm. She meant the world to Dave and me and was moved to tears when we told her that Nathan Kean Marrs would be her namesake.

At my twenty-eight-week appointment, I practically received a gold star for rule-following and healthy-baby-heartbeat status. I left the appointment beaming triumphantly; I was excelling at this whole growing-two-human-beings thing. That weekend, I was taking Bailey on a walk when I started to feel sluggish with a slight ache in my abdomen. I went to bed early that night and took it easy the rest of the week. On Thursday morning, I woke up with a dull stomachache that persisted all morning. I wasn't worried but decided to check in with my doctor just in case. He asked me to come by the clinic—I assumed he wanted to rule out a stomach virus or other illness.

At the doctor's office, I was shocked to find out that the pain I had been experiencing was contractions. I learned that I was dilated as the nurses hooked me up to two Doppler ultrasounds to monitor the boys' heartbeats and a tocodynamometer to measure the contractions. Within the hour, I was admitted to the hospital and moved to the labor and delivery unit. There, the nurses administered magnesium in an attempt to stop the contractions and a steroid shot to help kick-start the boys' lung development. As the day progressed, so did my labor. Within the next few hours, I dilated to four centimeters, and my contractions were coming faster and more regularly. I was overwhelmed and scared. As nurses scurried in and out of my room, it was as though I were watching a movie—nothing felt real. Dave was keeping my family in Florida updated by phone while his parents stood by my bedside, massaging my back and offering ice chips. The hospital chaplain came into my room and prayed with us and for us. We cried together, and I just kept begging God to protect my boys.

After nine hours, the attending doctor decided to transfer me by helicopter to the University of Arkansas for Medical Sciences hospital in Little Rock. We were told the boys would be arriving within the next twelve hours, and I needed to be at a hospital with the NICU capabilities to care for twenty-nine-week premature twin boys. The flight would save us nearly four hours of travel time. I shivered in fear, processing what this move meant.

As I was rolled onto the "Angel One" helicopter on the rooftop of Mercy Hospital in Rogers, I started having an adverse reaction to the high dosage of magnesium I'd been given. My body felt like it was on fire—every nerve burned, and my eyes couldn't focus. As I was losing consciousness, I clung to Dave and begged him to come on the helicopter with me. I refused to let go of his hand. Disregarding the strict policy that prohibits passengers on the helicopter with the patient, the pilot graciously allowed Dave to board with me.

The flight felt like it lasted hours. I was in and out of consciousness, and when I was awake, I begged God to protect my babies. I was so afraid the boys would be born in the air. When we finally landed, I remember being raced into the high-risk antepartum unit. People were shouting as lights streamed past me overhead. It was an out-of-body experience, and time felt strangely hurried while concurrently moving in slow motion.

Once I was settled in my room and hooked up to what felt like a dozen machines, the neonatologist came into the room to speak with us. She was primarily concerned with the development of the boys' lungs, as males are more likely to have pulmonary disorders associated with preterm birth. She went on to explain other potential complications, such as the chance the boys would be born blind. As she continued sharing the risks associated with premature male twins, I couldn't focus. She went hazy, and her words were incomprehensible to my ears. I will never be able to explain what happened, but I believe the Lord was protecting my heart from being burdened with her worst-case scenario speech. As she spoke, I felt an overwhelming sense of peace, and the words *They will be okay* resonated in my spirit. I didn't hear them aloud, but I have never been more confident of the voice of God.

When the doctor left the room, Dave turned to me with tears in his red-rimmed eyes. I assured him, "They're going to be okay. I know they will." He slowly nodded and asked if I would be all right if he left the room for a few minutes. I said I would and watched through the glass as my strong and steady husband crumpled to the floor just outside my hospital door.

As I sat in bed, unable to move, I talked to God. "They're yours, Lord. You brought us this far, and I know you've got them. They've always been yours. I love them so very much and I haven't even met them yet. I can't imagine how much you must love them if I feel this way. Can you please keep them safe in there for a while longer? Prove all of these doctors wrong. Please, Lord. Please."

Dave walked back into the room with his parents, who had just arrived. They told me my parents, siblings, and nephews were en route on the seventeen-hour drive from Florida. Dave explained that we needed to keep the boys in utero for ten more hours (to reach the required twenty-four-hour mark since our first steroid shot) in order for me to receive a second shot that would help their lungs develop. The medical team felt that making it to that point was highly unlikely due to how quickly my labor was progressing, but ten hours became our wild miracle goal. The boys needed that shot. The nurse came in every fifteen minutes to check on me and we collectively celebrated at every quarter-hour mark. They were still holding steady in utero.

Together with Dave, his parents, and his siblings, we held vigil. We prayed without ceasing and celebrated every milestone. Fifteen minutes, thirty minutes, one hour. I kept saying, "They're going to be okay. They're going to be okay." It was both a reminder and a desperate prayer.

My family arrived at four A.M. They raced into my room and huddled around my bed. We cried and hugged and prayed. Everyone who loved us and loved these two boys stood by my bedside and witnessed the miracles that would unfold over the next forty-eight hours. As we celebrated each hour, suddenly we looked at the clock and realized a full twenty-four hours had passed since I had checked in to Mercy Hospital.

At noon, the neonatologist came back into the room and smiled. We had made it. I received the second dose of steroids for the boys' lung development. As it was administered into my IV, I prayed that the Holy Spirit would fill the lungs of my boys with strength and might. I prayed that they would defy every odd we were given. I prayed that they would shout and jump and tumble like little boys do. I prayed that they would one day run around a track and play in a soccer game.

We continued to monitor the minutes and hours until we reached the forty-eight-hour mark when, mercifully, a nurse came into my room and announced I could finally have a cracker and some orange juice. That cracker tasted like manna from heaven. Within the next hour, my contractions miraculously subsided. I joked that the boys just needed a snack. Twenty-four hours later, our neonatologist came into the room and said, "I can't believe I'm saying this. But you are holding steady, and we are moving you from the high-risk unit and into a room on the general antepartum unit. I never thought you'd make it this far."

This felt like an enormous milestone, but we weren't out of the woods yet. Dr. Wendell, the doctor on call, came into my room and explained that I was not to do anything other than lie there calmly and be an incubator. Every hour we could keep the boys in utero was precious and desperately needed. I obliged and proceeded to watch my favorite rainy-day movie, *Under the Tuscan Sun,* no fewer than three times per day.

When we realized I'd be in the hospital longer-term, I went on temporary medical leave from my job and lay there all day, every day. Day and night, nurses would rotate in and out of the room, checking my vitals. Dave attempted to sleep on the hard sofa, and I struggled to get comfortable amidst all the wires and the weight of my now enormous belly. I was exhausted and antsy lying there without fresh air or freedom to come and go as I pleased. I missed my bed and desperately wanted to get home to finish decorating the nursery. I lamented the fact that I had missed my baby shower and pre-birthing class and never had a chance to take maternity photos.

Three weeks later, I was able to move from the hospital to a nearby hotel room. Even though I still reported back to the hospital multiple times a day, being out of the sterile environment lifted my spirits immensely.

After being in Little Rock for a month, I was given permission to travel back home while remaining on strict bed rest there. I was officially thirty-two weeks along, and our local NICU was now able to care for the boys if they were born prematurely. I was thrilled to be back in our own home. And then, less than one week later, the contractions started again, and I headed back to our local hospital. They quickly admitted me and started me on the protocol to attempt to keep the boys in utero as long as possible. I labored for forty-eight hours. Forty-eight more precious hours for the boys to develop and grow. Suddenly, the doctor announced it was time.

As I was wheeled into the OR (in case a C-section was needed), I held tightly to Dave's hand and suddenly realized aloud, "I didn't get a chance to take a birthing class. I don't know how to breathe or push!" Dave assured me that I knew how to breathe and that he would be right there with me. As I was being moved to the OR bed, I began spiraling into a full-blown panic. Dave gripped my face, looked into my eyes, and spoke in a confident, steady voice, "You can do this. I've seen how strong you are and how hard you've fought for our boys. Keep fighting."

Before I had time to think about it any longer, the on-call doctor announced it was time to push. I pushed and pushed and pushed. After an hour, I was losing strength. I hadn't eaten in over two days and had barely slept. After my next push, I looked at Dave and cried, "Something's wrong! I know it. Something's wrong."

My doctor agreed, and within seconds, a sterile drape was hung, orders were shouted, and I screamed as I felt the tension of a blade. Ben was pulled out first. Baby A. He was farthest into the birth canal but had been stuck.

With each push, his head collided with my pelvic bone. When he entered the world, I caught a quick glimpse, and my heart leapt. I didn't notice that he was blue. I didn't realize he never cried. Before I could understand what was happening, he was swept from the room by the neonatologist and a team of nurses. I turned to Dave, looking for reassurance that Ben was okay. Instead, he said, "Look! Nathan's here!" Nathan was screaming, and his skin was a healthy, vibrant shade of red. He was full of life. I watched helplessly as Dave cut the umbilical cord and carried Nathan over to me so I could see his precious face. I only had a moment with him before I saw the hospital chaplain enter the room and both Nathan and Dave were quickly escorted to the NICU. Before I could process what was happening, the world went black.

I awoke disoriented and in extreme pain. Seeing my eyes open, my mom leapt from the chair and came to my bedside. I immediately started shouting, "Where are they? Is Ben okay?! Mom, what's happening? Where's Dave?!" She explained that Dave was in the NICU with the boys, and Ben was on a CPAP machine. They had run a lot of tests. His head was swollen and bruised. My dad raced back into the room with Dave as he calmly explained what had happened. Ben had been stuck in the birth canal. He was having trouble breathing. I had to see them. Against the doctor's orders, I climbed out of bed and into a wheelchair, and Dave gently wheeled me into the NICU to see my boys. They were so small they could fit in the palm of Dave's hand. Ben was so bruised. There were so many wires and tubes. They were here, but this wasn't right. It wasn't supposed to be this way. They were supposed to be in my arms. I wept when I was told I couldn't hold them yet.

I was led back to my hospital room with instructions to pump so that the boys could be fed the vitally important, nutrient-dense colostrum. Afterward, I was mercifully allowed to hold Nathan while his first tube feed was administered. I marveled at every detail of his tiny body. I held his little hand with my finger as I rocked him in my arms. In that sterile atmosphere, with machines beeping and nurses surrounding me, I was on holy ground. My baby boys were here. We had fought so hard to get to this moment, and we would keep fighting to get them home.

After twenty-four hours, Ben was taken off the CPAP machine, and I was allowed to hold him. My tears freely fell as the nurse placed him in my arms. Dave was sitting in the chair beside me, holding Nathan. We were both in absolute awe looking at these miraculous little fighters. They were completely healthy, yet they would need to learn how to eat because they had been born before the suck-breathe-swallow function had developed in utero. That was it. After every worst-case scenario had been given, we just had to let them grow and learn to eat. Miracle upon miracle upon miracle.

One month after Ben and Nathan entered the world, we hugged the NICU nurses and walked out of the hospital for the first time as a family of four. I sat in the back between the two car seats and reminded Dave to drive carefully. We pulled into our driveway and were greeted by our cheering family members. They held a large banner that simply and poignantly stated, "Welcome Home, Ben and Nathan!"

We walked inside, carrying car seats holding our sleeping boys, and set them down on the kitchen floor next to their four-months-older cousin. My sister-in-law stood beside me as we marveled at our three babies together. Exactly one year after I had sat on that same kitchen floor and cried under the crushing weight of grief, I now stood and celebrated the abundant faithfulness of God as I snapped a photo of the three newest additions to the Marrs family.

CHAPTER 6

SEEING HER FACE

One night, in the years before the twins were born, I awoke disoriented from a vivid dream. Dave and I were standing at the kitchen island, surrounded by the joyful chaos of kids running around us, shrieking and giggling. I felt deep contentment as the sounds of life and laughter enveloped us. I distinctly remember the features of two of the children while the others ran past in a beautiful blur. One was a towheaded boy, and the other was a dark-skinned little girl with puffs of hair in twin pigtails. Despite my grogginess, I was keenly aware this dream was significant. I shook Dave awake and told him that one of our children would be born in Africa. He was confused by my odd middle-of-the-night proclamation. We both went back to sleep and forgot all about that dream until many years later.

The twins were not quite eighteen months old when I felt a gentle stirring in my spirit. Dave and I had begun the adoption process before I was pregnant with the boys and had placed our file on hold when I found out I was expecting. I now sensed it was time to move forward, but I didn't want to tell Dave because, although I was certain this was what God was calling our family toward, I wanted to ensure we were on the same page. Our boys were so little, and we were barely keeping our heads above water with the needs of twin toddlers, lack of sleep, and full-time jobs.

On a beautiful spring day in early March, I loaded the boys into the double stroller and headed to the park. As we walked down the driveway, Dave's truck pulled in, and he asked me to wait so he could come with us. As I pushed the stroller, Dave nonchalantly announced, "I feel like we are supposed to start the adoption process again."

My skin tingled as goosebumps covered my arms. I stopped walking, looked him in the eye, and replied simply and confidently, "Me too."

We knew enough about the process to know that it would not be easy. We spent the next few months researching and meeting with dozens of domestic and international adoption agencies, as well as adoptive and foster families. When we began our paperwork, there were days when I felt so overwhelmed that I would find myself staring at the checklists of requirements through frustrated tears. Yet, we knew that we had been called to this path by a God who had repeatedly proven Himself faithful. We could trust that if He wanted us to bring a child into our family through adoption, He would make a way. We could confidently step forward in surrendered faith.

The next seven months were spent completing dozens of government forms, attending training sessions, obtaining fingerprint appointments and background checks. We compiled a giant stack of paperwork to create our adoption dossier and were officially placed on our agency's waiting list. At that point, we were told it could be another eighteen months before we were matched with a child. This seemed to uncover why we felt the need to start the process when we did. On this timeline, the boys would be four years old before a potential brother or sister joined our family.

Each month, we received updated wait-list numbers. These numbers reflected our proximity to a referral (a match, in adoption terms). On the day that marked one year on the wait list, I felt an overwhelming sense that our child was out there in the world waiting for us. I am still not quite sure how to put what I felt into words. I can only liken it to how I felt when I first heard the twins' heartbeats: *I am a momma.* And I had the same feeling on that October morning. Soon after, I wrote these words to our child, even though I didn't know who he or she was or where he or she was in the world. My momma's heart knew.

Dearest one,

You are already loved deeply and fervently. In ordinary moments, I find myself aching for you. Walking to the park with your brothers, I imagine holding you in my arms. Sitting in a church pew, I dream about introducing you to the church family who prays for you alongside us. Shopping at the grocery store, I wonder if you'll eat handfuls of "boo-boo-berries" and frozen grapes like your brothers.

Please know that you are prayed for and loved and wanted. While we wait here to know you, I can trust that your Heavenly Father knows your story. He knows the heartache and pain and loss you will endure. He will hold you and He will protect you. He will sing calming songs over you. He will be there even if we can't. I trust in Him. I know His plans for your life are far greater than anything I could even begin to imagine or dream up on my own. He loves you even more than I can fathom. He will bring you here to our family in His time. He will heal your heart, and He will restore your life. He will guide your daddy and me and teach us how to best care for you. He will show us how to pick up the shattered pieces of your heart and lovingly mend the brokenness. He will make us a family.

We love you and cannot wait to meet you, precious one.

All my love,
Your Momma

As I penned this letter to my child, I had no way of knowing what events were unfolding half a world away. I had no way of knowing that on that very day, as I sat in my chair by the window writing in my journal, my baby girl was becoming the newest resident in an overrun, under-resourced orphanage in the Congo.

Exactly one month after writing that letter, on Monday, November 12, I received an email from a waiting-child adoption website. Upon opening it, I was greeted by a photo of a nine-month-old baby girl named Sylvie. She had been placed on the site about an hour before, and as I read her information, I felt an undeniable urge to call Dave to tell him about her. At his prompting to know more, I raced across town to meet him in front of a job-site, where I showed him her photo. Our hearts were stirred—"stirred" is a nice, easy word, but it's not the right one . . . I don't know what the right one is . . . "broken," "overwhelmed," "wrecked"—as we gazed into her big brown eyes. Her button nose and pinchable cheeks tugged at our hearts. We prayed together in the car. We begged for discernment and clarity. Is this our daughter, Lord? Is she the one we have been waiting for?

We agreed that we should get more information about her. At this point, we didn't know which country she lived in, only that she was in Africa. After talking with her agency, we learned more about her story, including the fact that she was in the Democratic Republic of the Congo and that forty other families had inquired. We prayed and discussed what we should do. We started researching her country and the agency. Because our current agency focused on adoptions from Ethiopia, we knew that if we officially accepted Sylvie's referral, we would have to start over with a new agency and a new country program. This meant that all of our current paperwork and the money we had already paid would be gone. Even so, we both felt like she was the one. We had to decide quickly, so the next day, we called the agency and told them that we wanted to adopt Sylvie. We were the first qualifying family to say yes to our girl, and her file was put on hold until we submitted our official referral paperwork and payment.

Almost immediately, I connected with several families adopting through this new agency and program. These families shared very hard stories about the orphanage where Sylvie was living and warned us that adoptions from the Congo were very risky. We were advised again and again to be cautious and to do our research before proceeding. I was on the phone until midnight with a new friend in Oklahoma who shared her story with me, and after hanging up from that phone call, I was heartbroken, confused, and scared to move forward. I didn't know if God was answering my prayers for clarity with this phone call or if it was fear trying to deter us from our path.

The next morning, Dave and I agreed that we felt an intense unease and decided that we should not proceed. Instead, we would stay on our path of working with our current agency. My heart was shattered. We planned to call the agency after Dave got home from work to let them know.

Dave arrived home later than planned, and when he walked in the door, he asked, "So, what are we going to do?" My emotions nearly boiled over. We had made a decision, and I was trying impossibly hard to be at peace with that decision. Now Dave had opened the door just enough for me to see the light of hope shine through. He knew I was ready to move forward if he was. But only if we were on the same page. God knew we needed full assurance to move forward. He knew we were stepping onto a spiritual battlefield by saying yes. He knew we would need markers of His faithfulness to sustain us on the journey ahead.

Dave then shared how, earlier in the day, he had unexpectedly received a call from a friend and business partner about a closing he had forgotten about. They had sold a parcel of land and needed to sign the final paperwork. Dave left that meeting with a check for nearly the exact amount we would need for Sylvie's referral payment—a rather significant amount of money. The payment was something we had questioned and prayed about. We had been unsure where we would find the money in three days when we hadn't planned for this referral. We both felt that this was God's hand, and we could not ignore His provision. This was Wednesday evening, and we had until Friday to make our decision.

I spent several hours on Thursday in a gorgeous glass chapel that sits on the top of a hill near our home. I prayed and read scripture, particularly the book of Isaiah. I was reminded again and again that God is good.

Fear and doubt and confusion are *not* from Him. He is bigger than a corrupt government or orphanage director. He is bigger than the risks. He is the same God of miracles today that He was in the Old Testament.

During my time in that little chapel, I remembered that Dave and I had long ago surrendered our family at God's feet. He had slowly, thoughtfully, and perfectly shown us His plan for us over time. If I had been told ten years before that I would spend thousands of dollars and an unknown amount of time to attempt to bring a little girl home from a war-torn country in the depths of poverty and corruption to become our daughter, I would have been overwhelmed, to say the least. Yet, today, here I stood. Still overwhelmed but wholly trusting and confident that He is good and He is able.

I called Dave from the chapel and told him that I believed Sylvie was our daughter, and we had to try to get her home, even if it would be scary and risky and dangerous. Even if we had no guarantee that she would ever come home. We had to try. We couldn't turn away.

Dave agreed.

At the time, I had no way of knowing how impossibly hard the road to bring Sylvie home would be. Yet I knew she was mine, and I was hers. I had fallen in love with our girl through a couple of photographs and a longing to know her. Just as a pregnant mother doesn't know her child's personality or temperament or what he or she will feel like in her arms, she knows that she loves this child with every fiber of her being. That was where I was. I prayed for her when I woke up in the morning and in whispers throughout the day. I prayed for her at mealtimes, fervently pleading that she was being fed. I prayed for her as I cuddled our boys at night, beseeching our God to ensure that she was being held and comforted when she cried. I prayed for her as I lay my head on my pillow at night, asking that she was safe as she slept. Above all, I knew she was my daughter, and I would fight with all I had to bring her home. And, it turns out, that was exactly what I would need to do.

CHAPTER 7

MY BOLD PRAYER

Our dining room table was covered in two stacks of papers at all times: newly updated documents and still-needing-to-be-updated documents. The papers taunted me as a new sense of urgency mounted: We had a daughter. Sylvie was halfway around the globe, and I had no way of knowing if she was safe.

The steps ahead of us were clear, if not simple. Once we completed our dossier, we would submit it, and then the local commune in Kinshasa would meet to determine if Sylvie's case was cleared for adoption. After numerous court hearings, court-approved documents and adoption decrees would be issued, passports and visas would be secured for Sylvie, and, finally, an exit permit would grant permission for her to leave the country.

The process was painstakingly slow. Communication was sparse and infrequent. Updates were minimal. I checked my email day and night. If an email came across from the agency, I rushed to open it. Two months after we said yes, a new set of photos arrived in my inbox. They felt like a treasure. The photos were proof: She is real, she is alive. Dave and I studied and memorized every single detail of the photos. We hung one on the wall and clung to the hope that it provided. Hope that our girl was healthy and safe. She had changed so much since we first saw her face two months before. I was shocked at how fast she was growing.

In February, the U.S. Embassy in the Democratic Republic of the Congo declared that adoptive families should anticipate a three-to-six-month lag time in the process. We now had no way of knowing if Sylvie would come home within the year.

Twelve days after the announcement, I awoke to an email with news that Sylvie had malaria. One of the other moms adopting through our agency had connected with a local Congolese doctor, Dr. Laure, through a missionary living in the DRC. The two had stayed in touch and, at the request of myself and a couple of other parents with children at the same orphanage, Dr. Laure had visited the orphanage the day prior. I felt confident that we would get a happy, healthy report. We'd even received a photo the day before where Sylvie was *almost* smiling. I thought she looked happy for the first time since we had seen her face.

After reading the report in the email, I took another look at the photo where I thought Sylvie might be smiling and, this time, I noticed that she looked more like she was wincing and pulling back. How could I have mistaken the two so easily?

After the boys went down for their afternoon nap, I took a shower and sobbed as the water poured over my back. I pleaded with God to show me that He was protecting Sylvie. After my shower, I felt led to pick up my journal and read through notes I'd taken at an adoptive mom retreat I'd attended earlier in the month. The speaker on Sunday morning had walked us through the story of Hagar in Genesis, and this passage jumped out at me:

God heard the boy crying, and the angel of God called to Hagar from heaven and said to her, "What is the matter, Hagar? Do not be afraid; God has heard the boy crying as he lies there." (Genesis 21:17, NIV)

Then, underneath, I had written: "The same God who heard the cries of Hagar's son hears the cries of my Sylvie. I feel like God is saying to me, *I hear the cries of Sylvie right where she is. Remember my faithfulness.*"

I read my own words and felt an indescribable peace and reassurance that God was with us in this fight. I heard the boys rustle from sleep and ascended the stairs to lift their warm, still-sleepy selves from their toddler beds. As I did so, I whispered a prayer of gratitude for my boys and a prayer of protection for my girl.

Two days later, I received an update that Sylvie's health was improving. As I rejoiced in this update, I received another email with a description of the type of orphanage Sylvie was living in. It was overcrowded and run-down, without running water or electricity. After reading these descriptions, I felt led to pray specifically for Sylvie to be home by June. By human accounts, this was impossible. I emailed my agency representative with my goal for June. She told me there was absolutely no way this could happen. I remained undeterred. My prayer was for June. I reminded myself that God was fighting for Sylvie. He can make the impossible possible.

One month later, in mid-April, our case was still awaiting a court date. We were stuck in limbo. Sylvie had been in and out of the hospital again, and I feared for her safety every single moment of every single day. In my desperation, I wrote to my girl in the pink-and-white journal I kept for her, recording the details of our wait.

To my precious Sylvie,

I know you don't know about me just yet. Your sweet, strong daddy reminds me of this in (failed) attempts to comfort my breaking heart. He reminds me that although I ache for you with a desperation that words cannot possibly give appropriate credit to, you are not crying out for me in the night. You are not crying yourself to sleep pleading to God to move swiftly on your behalf. You are not hoping for a life here in our family. Yet, here I am. Doing all of those things. I pace the floors of our home, circling the room where you will one day lay your sweet head, pleading to my Heavenly Father to bring you here to us quickly. I hope against hope that He will move mountains on your behalf.

Today, I took an innocent walk over to the baby aisle while picking up a few groceries and found myself unable to see clearly through my tears. I was overcome with emotion as I contemplated all of the food available to growing bellies. I knew that you were not receiving any of these things.

Ultimately, simple rice cereal sent me over the edge. I was buying some to send with a traveling momma at the request of Dr. Laure, yet I wasn't sure what kind of cereal they would feed you at the orphanage. I wasn't sure if they would sell it the way they sold all of the other items I sent for you last time. I wasn't sure what you were eating. I wasn't sure if you were eating. Most of all, I wasn't sure how I could stand there, in that aisle, with all of the selections, knowing that the possibility of your little tummy rumbling from hunger was undeniable.

This wait for you is the hardest, most torturous, gut-wrenching thing I have ever had to do in my life. I am grieving for you. I want you to understand that you are wanted. I want you to know that you are loved. I want you to be here, laughing and smiling. I want to see a light in those big, dark eyes.

I cry out to God, again and again, questioning WHY you are there, WHY you are so sick, WHY you are stuck in a system that makes no sense to me.

And, again and again, I ask that He use all of this pain, all of this hurt, all of this grief. All of the loss you are enduring. All of the fear and confusion and brokenness.

All of it.

For His glory.

He makes ALL things beautiful, my love. Even all of this. This is not too much for Him. This is not out of His reach. He is sovereign. His love is all-consuming. He holds this whole world in His hands. This whole wide world.

I'm steadfastly praying for your heart, precious one. I'm praying for angel armies to continue to surround and protect you. I'm praying Jesus will continue to whisper your name in the Heavens, and He will continue to hold your hand.

This beautiful story is still being written, even if I am anxious to turn to the next page.

Stay strong, sweet one. Hold on.

All my love,
Your Momma

We finally received word that our adoption case had passed court on May 27, 2013. At this point, we would begin the thirty-day wait for guardianship, after which we could wait anywhere from six to ten months to bring her home. The June homecoming I had continued to pray for was impossible.

Two weeks later, I was awakened in the night by a petrifying, gripping sense of fear. It felt as though someone was sitting on my chest; I swatted at what felt like hands around my throat. The air was dripping with darkness, and I immediately started praying. I strained to whisper the only word I could muster at that moment, "Jesus." Eventually, I was able to breathe. My body was left trembling. I couldn't get back to sleep and decided to check my emails. There was an email waiting from Dr. Laure: She now had Sylvie safely in her home! She had been able to move her from the orphanage after an intense argument with the orphanage director. The director did not want to let her go, fearing the money I sent each month would no longer come. It was abundantly clear that she didn't care about Sylvie, only money. I had assured the director the week before, when Dr. Laure had first discussed the possibility of fostering Sylvie, that I would still pay our monthly orphanage fee even if Sylvie wasn't living there. I wanted her in Laure's home—where she would be loved, cared for, and safe. I looked at the time of the email: ten A.M. in the DRC. The moment Sylvie left the orphanage gates was three A.M. CST—the same time I was awakened by intense fear.

Evil did not win.

The next day, I received updated photos from Dr. Laure. Sylvie had been given medicine and was eating a hot meal. My heart rejoiced, and I exhaled in deep relief. Sylvie was not in my home, but she was now in a loving foster home. Dr. Laure would stand in the gap for me. She would love her in the in-between. Sylvie was in a place where she would receive love, care, and nutrition. She was in a place where she was safe. My bold prayer for June was, in fact, answered.

CHAPTER 8

IN MY ARMS

As soon as Sylvie was declared our legal daughter, I booked flights for Dave and me to travel to the DRC to meet her in person. Although we didn't yet have the clearance to bring her home, we couldn't wait a moment longer to be on the same soil as our girl and hold her for the first time. In the days leading up to our departure, we were blessed by the generosity of family and friends who gave us medical supplies, infant formula, vitamins, clothes, toys, backpacks, and soccer balls, which we packed in our luggage alongside care packages sent by other parents for their children in the orphanage. I had packed several of my own care packages for our daughter and sent them with traveling families during the past nine months. I knew these packages contained items carefully chosen, prayed over, and shipped off with the hope that they would bring smiles and joy to their little ones.

After twenty-six hours of travel, we arrived in Kinshasa late at night. I had been warned that the airport would be frantic and could be one of the more dangerous areas we would visit. I was overwhelmed by the presence of armed guards, as well as the voices shouting in a foreign tongue and the general sense of chaos. We were exhausted as we waited at the luggage carousel for bags that never arrived.

The drive to Dr. Laure's home was long and allowed us to take in Kinshasa. Crowds of people were walking and talking alongside the highway. In the distance, the rhythm of music filled the air. Trucks passed, crammed with passengers, many with men hanging out the doors. A combination of dirt and diesel fumes hung in the stale night air. Roadside stands were lit by a single candle. Young men carried bags of cold drinks along the highway for those waiting in the seemingly never-ending lines of traffic. Each time we passed a woman on the street with a baby strapped to her back or a mother holding a sleeping infant while selling vegetables from a small stand, I thought of Sylvie's birth mother. I wondered about her life. I wondered what she had experienced and what hardships she had endured. I pondered the chain of events that had caused our worlds to collide, bringing Dave and me to this place, loving the little girl she had carried in her womb. I was on the brink of tears throughout the long, silent drive.

When we arrived at Dr. Laure's home, her entire family rushed out to greet us in the driveway with the most heartfelt, kind, and warm welcome. After hugging each of Laure's six adorable, energetic children, I looked up and saw Sylvie. She was carried outside by Laure's sister, Linda, and she was sound asleep. I had imagined this moment so many times, and I was anxious about how she would react to us. When I learned we would be arriving at night, I thought there could be a possibility of meeting her for the first time while she was asleep, which would allow me to hold her without her being afraid. And that's how it happened: an answered prayer. I stared at her and whispered, "You are so beautiful, my sweet girl!" I couldn't believe she was in my arms at last.

Our first morning together began early. We were worried Sylvie would scream or cry when she awoke, but she simply blinked at us and didn't make a sound. We quickly learned that she had a freeze response to fear.

We gently gave her the light-up glowworm toy her brothers had sent for her, and she just stared at it and held it close. Slowly, we made our way outside to the front patio before everyone else woke up, and there, she let me hold her and rock her. Eventually, she gave me a tentative smile, and I heard her beautiful laugh for the first time. My heart was full.

When Laure's mom, Meme, arrived, Sylvie no longer wanted me near. Meme was the one taking care of Sylvie most days, and Sylvie pushed me away and screamed if I tried to hold her. I knew to expect this, but it still broke my heart and made me long for the day when she could trust me.

That afternoon, Dr. Laure drove Dave and me to the airport to try to retrieve our lost luggage. We spent four hours waiting and when our bags finally arrived, we were deeply grateful. As we walked out, we were stopped by armed guards who proceeded to search each bag and take whatever they wanted for themselves. The deflated soccer balls, hand pumps, and baby formula were all taken. I tried to explain these were for the orphanage but was quickly dismissed. Eventually, Dr. Laure came inside to find us and saw the guards ransacking our belongings. She confronted them, and an intense shouting match began. We tried to explain that it was okay, she didn't need to argue with them, we just wanted to get out of there. She was undeterred and unafraid of the AK-47s strapped to the chests of the officers. She stood her ground, and although we didn't get our belongings returned, we were allowed to leave with the items we still had left. This would be the first of several times throughout our visit Dr. Laure would have to stand up to officers. Her courage, tenacity, and grace astounded me. She never flinched. She never shrank back. She confidently held her head high and refused to be coerced. I whispered many prayers of gratitude that our daughter was being cared for by this strong and Godly woman as we waited to bring her home.

We planned to visit Sylvie's former orphanage after leaving the airport. It was located deep in the slums of Kinshasa, and as we drove through the dirt roads covered in mounds of trash and animal waste, we inhaled the fumes of diesel, charcoal, and thick smog. I badly wanted to take a photo, but doing so in public as a foreigner was illegal. I knew my mental images would be all I had to carry home with me. I attempted to commit to memory the image of the little boy running through the dirt with his handmade stick car being pulled by a tattered twine rope. I observed the women balancing heavy buckets on their heads while they carried young children on their backs. I desperately tried to absorb the sights, sounds, and smells. I wanted to remember every detail of Sylvie's birth country to share with her as she grew up.

As we inched closer to Sylvie's orphanage, I knew that we were passing the streets where our daughter spent her first months on this earth. My heart ached as I gazed out the window of our van. I had to remind myself to breathe as I watched this world, her world, pass by. We got out of the car and stepped through the worn metal gate, welcomed in a flurry of excitement by dozens of outstretched ebony arms. The deafening silence on the other side of the concrete wall was instantly replaced with shrieks of laughter and soft-spoken greetings.

I was struck by how this small compound with two concrete buildings framing a dirt courtyard in the center was no place for a child. There wasn't any grass for playing, only coarse dirt that stained the soles of the children's bare feet and created a dusty film over every surface. Children slept on concrete floors, and a handful of holes in the ground served as restrooms for the fifty-four children living there.

Almost immediately, I saw the future daughter of another mom who was adopting through our agency. She was five or six years old, rail-thin, with haunted, hollow eyes. She waited for the other children to scatter before quietly approaching me, a faint smile forming on her lips. I reached out and clasped her sharp, bony hands in my own as I kneeled to her level. I was told her name was Harper. I didn't speak Lingala, and she didn't speak English. Yet, I believed she understood as I told her how honored I was to meet her.

Harper never left my side. As Dave and I listened to the children singing, she stood near me. As I passed out snacks, she held her head low and would steal glances my way. While the boys played soccer with Dave, she sat right next to me on the concrete porch, our legs dangling over the edge and my arm wrapped around her frail body as she leaned into my embrace. She was desperate for attention and, mostly, for love. I showered her with affection during my short stay, hoping this feeble offering of love would sustain her after I left.

As dusk was settling, we said our goodbyes. I held Harper in my arms and whispered a prayer into her ear. Tears pooled in my eyes as we exited the gate. I knew the children would face another night in pitch blackness without electricity. My heart broke knowing they would huddle together on the hard floor to face the darkness.

Dave and I were silent during the drive back to Laure's home. The extremely under-resourced orphanage had been our own daughter's home for the first year and a half of her life. Dave and I sat in the back of the van, our eyes glistening as we held tightly to each other's hands.

The faces of the children we met were now seared into our minds, and we knew our lives were forever changed.

After the long drive back home, we arrived to find Sylvie in the kitchen eating dinner. I approached her slowly and tried to greet her. In return, I received shrieks and tears. I knew this was normal, but still, I went to our room, collapsed on the bed, and let the tears I had been holding in since we arrived flow freely. Dave quietly entered and sat next to me, rubbing my back as I cried, feeling broken and desperate. Eventually, I took a deep breath, sat up, and we prayed together. Words fell short. We simply prayed, "Jesus, be near." After dinner, Sylvie took a little nap, which we were told did not normally happen in the evening, granting us time to hold her in our arms. I sang to my girl and prayed over her. "Lord, I know that Sylvie may feel overwhelmed and scared right now. Let her feel our love, both while we are here and once we return home. Keep her safe in your protective embrace."

Over the course of our visit, Sylvie's fears slowly dissipated and were replaced with a tentative curiosity. She'd watch as Laure's children laughed and danced with Dave and me each evening after dinner. Eventually, she started to learn that these new people in her life were safe, and she would join us on our makeshift living room dance floor. She laughed while applying stickers to Dave's face and arms and giggled as I painted her nails the bright pink shade she'd chosen from the nail polish I had brought for Laure's older daughters. We'd spend hot afternoons drawing pictures together on the terrace. She'd crawl into my lap and listen intently as I read the books I had brought for her. Each morning, I fed her breakfast and her raspy laughter punctuated the sweltering air as I played the "airplane spoon" game her brothers had always loved so much. On our last afternoon, we had to drive to the airline's downtown office to check in before our flight that evening. Sylvie fell asleep on the long journey and, as I held her, I studied her features and committed the weight of her small body in my arms to memory. After checking in, we went to a nearby restaurant for dinner, where Sylvie sat in my lap and let me feed her. She was content while I simultaneously felt deep joy and deep dread.

After dinner, as we drove to the airport, Sylvie snuggled against my chest. Holding her against me, I gave in to the tears that had threatened all day. Once we arrived and stepped outside, I could hardly breathe. None of this felt real. I had to leave my baby girl behind. I clung to her until the last possible moment. Laure gently peeled Sylvie from my arms, looking into my eyes and repeating, "I'm so sorry. I'm so sorry." Dave held me up, and I kept my eyes locked on Sylvie the entire time we walked toward the door. I didn't look away until we turned a corner to enter the security line.

The room spun, and my head felt dizzy. My vision blurred as the tears streamed. As Dave and I sat in the stale, oppressively hot airport terminal, I felt numb. I couldn't believe we had to go home without our daughter. I tried to remind myself that we had made progress on the visit. After a meeting with the U.S. Embassy, we were told we should anticipate a month, maybe two, until we could return and bring her home for good. One month. Maybe two. We could make it.

As the plane ascended and I watched Sylvie's homeland fade from view, I took a deep breath and resolved once again to hand over control to God's capable hands. I repeated the same four words I had desperately uttered countless times on this journey: "I trust you, Jesus."

CHAPTER 9

THE IN-BETWEEN

One month after returning home from the Congo, we loaded the car with suitcases and our rambunctious three-year-old boys and drove thirteen hours to the beach on the edge of Florida's Panhandle for a weeklong vacation with my parents. When we'd planned this vacation the year before, we were certain that Sylvie would be home and this would be our first vacation together as a family of five. I had conjured images in my mind of what this week would look like: Sylvie and the boys playing together in the sand for the first time as brothers and sister, the three of them bonding while jumping waves and swimming in the pool. Driving there without her felt all wrong.

On the first morning, I tiptoed out to the back deck with a steaming mug cupped between my hands so I could watch the sunrise and listen to the waves crashing along the shore. Standing there, feeling small against the vastness of the ocean before me, I took a deep breath and wondered if maybe, just maybe, the verse I'd been clinging to during our adoption process—Ephesians 3:20—was just as true now as it was when it was written almost two thousand years ago. Maybe God's plans could be greater than I could even imagine. I felt a stirring in my spirit, a gentle nudge to trust that He was moving in a way I couldn't fully understand.

The house inside was quiet. The boys were still asleep, giving me time to process all that had happened in the past few days. Earlier in the week, when I needed to run to the drugstore while the boys were at preschool, I had a very random urge to buy a pregnancy test. Never in a million years did I think it would be positive. I didn't even know why I was buying it. I hadn't bought one in over four years and had no reason to buy one now. The doctors had made it crystal clear that I could never get pregnant without medical intervention. It was impossible. But, still, I picked up the box and carried it to the front register.

I came home and took the test right away. Checked it. Washed my hands. Checked again. One line. Done. I went on with my day and started cleaning up the dishes in the kitchen sink.

About five minutes later, I felt a little nudge. Maybe I should have waited the full two minutes recommended on the box before checking the results . . . but no. It wouldn't have made a difference . . . or . . . would it? I walked back to the bathroom for a quick check and squealed loudly when I saw the two pink lines. I was shocked. I gulped down another glass of water, took the other test in the box . . . waited two minutes . . . and then proceeded to hyperventilate.

I called Dave and told him to meet me outside the house he was working on because I had something to show him. He later told me that he thought I had an email saying we could go get Sylvie—he never would have guessed what I had to share instead. He met me outside and I showed him the two tests. He started laughing deeply from a well of joy.

The next day, we left for the beach. Now, standing at the edge of the sea, questions were whirling through my mind. I couldn't understand why I would finally, miraculously, be pregnant *now,* as we were working so hard to get our daughter home. I wondered: What will happen when Sylvie comes home? Will the baby cause more confusion for her? Will she think she's being replaced? How will Sylvie and I bond while I care for a newborn? Will the timing work out? If Sylvie came home within the next month, that would give us approximately seven months of bonding before the baby arrived, which seemed doable. But, but . . . this was not in *my* plan.

As the questions swirled, I sat down and took out my journal. The words flowed onto the page without my even thinking about what I was writing: *This is not a surprise to God. He saw this coming.*

Later that day, we shared the news with my parents. They shrieked with delight. We all recognized this pregnancy as miraculous and incredible. Later, I'd learn this newest babe was a girl. Two girls. A double portion, once again. It was more beautiful and wonderful than I could have ever imagined.

On our last evening in Florida, my phone started buzzing incessantly. I glanced at the lit-up screen as I chopped cucumbers for a salad. I quickly wiped my hands on a nearby dish towel and answered. One of my fellow Congo-adoptive mom friends, Melanie, was on the line and flatly said, "Read your email right now. This is bad."

My hands shook as I hung up the phone and left the room. Dave glanced my way and, seeing my bottom lip trembling, knew that something was wrong. He followed me into the next room, where I opened the email app on my phone and waited impatiently for the newest messages to load. Then, it appeared:

The United States State Department Alert: *Democratic Republic of the Congo Immigration Authorities Suspend Issuance of Exit Permits to Adoptees.*

The email went on to explain that the immigration authorities in the Democratic Republic of the Congo had announced a suspension of exit permits to adoptees for up to twelve months. At this point, Sylvie was legally our daughter, and after obtaining her U.S. visa, the final document we needed for her to be allowed to leave her birth country was her exit permit. This suspension meant she couldn't leave the country for up to twelve months. I processed this news and felt the nausea churn in my stomach.

I wish I could say that I felt the quiet assurance of trust that God was in control even in this situation. But at that moment, I felt only fear and anger and confusion. Sylvie had been hospitalized with malaria and typhoid fever multiple times. She also had asthma, and it often escalated. We feared every day for her life. How could she wait another twelve months?

Dave held me as I cried into his chest. We didn't want to worry the boys, so we took a deep breath and quietly walked back into the kitchen, where my mom was bringing the salad to the table. Both she and my dad glanced at our faces and immediately knew something was wrong. I clenched my jaw and offered a sad smile, one that did not quite reach my eyes. After dinner, my mom offered to clean the dishes, and I found a quiet spot to read the book I had been prompted to pull off the shelf just before leaving for this trip, *Always True: God's 5 Promises When Life Is Hard* by James MacDonald.

I opened to the page I had left off on and found MacDonald's words echoing my heartache. "Christians don't generally set out to doubt God. We don't question our faith without reason. Life's pain or unexpected questions simply catch us off guard."

Caught off guard, indeed.

Tossing in the proverbial waves at the edge of the literal sea, I was feeling hopeless as I read these words: "The one who doubts is like a wave of the sea, blown and tossed by the wind" (James 1:6, NIV). I tried to pray, but all I could muster was a simple, sincere cry: "*Jesus, make a way where I can't see a way.*"

We arrived home without clarity or answers. Even

still, I decided to steadfastly trust that God—the One who had called us to this place, the One who had provided time and again, the One who had affirmed our path over and over—*would* move in a mighty way. He would protect our daughter and the other children who were stuck in the process along with her. He would hold her in His loving embrace. He would command His angel armies to surround her. He would protect her from illness. He would carry her home to Dave and me, and her brothers and sister-on-the-way, and aunts and uncles and nanas and grandpas who were all waiting and loving her from afar. Hope *would* rise.

Six weeks later, we were granted Sylvie's United States visa. This should have been a moment of rejoicing and celebrating and frantic packing and car-seat purchasing and last-minute room preparations. And yet. We continued to wait. We had no idea how much longer this waiting would last. Some days were so full of hope and anticipation of the miracle in store—every fiber of my being knew that the moment was coming soon when that plane would touch down on U.S. soil with our daughter tucked safely inside. On other days, the possibility seemed ridiculous and naive, and I allowed myself to wallow in the fact that the innocent prayers of my three-year-olds for their "sister to come home soon" might never happen.

On November 21, 2013, 374 days after we first saw our daughter's face, I wrote in my journal:

Today is an in-between day. Not full of hope. Not in the pit of despair. Just breathing. Continuing to stand in this in-between place. In-between the plans for the future. In-between plans for the holidays. Will we travel to Florida to visit family or stay home because of the possibility that a miracle could happen and we could bring Sylvie home? Should I finish decorating her room or just leave the piles of clothes, toys, and boxes for another day? It feels too much to ponder today. I'm thankful for her visa. I'm thankful for another step behind us. Yet, the clock is ticking until this document expires. In the meantime, we will wait. We will hold on to hope.

After writing these words, I reminded myself that we had been here before. In the in-between. In the waiting. We waited for three long years with empty arms, and God did not disappoint. He gave us overflowing arms and abundantly full hearts when our boys were born. Every tear on that journey was worth it. And now, despite all of the uncertainty, I had to trust that someday I would look back on this wait for our daughter and say the very same thing: *Every tear on this journey was worth it.*

CHAPTER 10

UNEXPECTED GIFTS

As the wait for Sylvie dragged from months to years, my weariness felt like a heavy cloak I slipped on each morning and carried throughout each day. I scribbled in my journal: *I want to sell everything. Or, better yet, I'll give it away. I need to free up space around me.* With the words came an unexpected realization: This wasn't simply about my stuff, this was about my life. I was exhausted and depleted. Something had to give.

I'd come to see that this shift was a call to be fully present for the ones under my roof. I had been living for too long with my heart divided between two continents. An onslaught of fears would overwhelm me even in the mundane moments of ordinary life. In the produce section of the grocery store, I would weep uncontrollably, wondering if Sylvie had eaten that day. As I tucked my boys into bed at night, my thoughts would always turn to our girl. Although Sylvie was now living in a foster home, Dr. Laure was a single mom with six children of her own, and due to the exit permit suspension, she had taken in another eight foster kids. I wondered: *Has Sylvie been held today? Is she sleeping in a bed tonight or on a cold floor? Does she still have the blanket I gave her on our last visit, or has it been confiscated by one of the older children?* The questions were relentless. The answers were elusive.

I thought back to the sunny December afternoon two years before when Dave had led the boys, then eighteen months old, and me over a grassy field and up rickety steps leading to the back door of an old home he had been hired to demolish. He pulled a key from his pocket and led us inside. The gleam in his eye was hard to miss as he walked from room to room describing the possibilities for the space: remove this wall, move this door here, replace that wall with windows, reconfigure the kitchen layout, replace the spiral staircase with a wooden one, and on and on. The project seemed immense. Yet the house exuded character and a hospitable charm, and as we toured it, I looked at Dave and said, "I can't bear to see this house torn down. What can we do?"

He explained his desire to save the home and how he had convinced the seller to agree to a trade. Rather than destroy the home, he would move it and clear the land in exchange for the deed. They had agreed, as the move saved thousands of dollars in demolition costs. After the move, we would restore and sell the house.

The plan seemed foolproof until he learned of an ordinance preventing the move of any home within city limits. After chuckling at such a bizarre ordinance (was there a time when homes were moved around town too often?), we were left feeling rather defeated. We had this gorgeous old home in need of restoration, ready and waiting to be moved. Yet the downtown lot we had planned to use for it was no longer an option.

We realized the hand of fate was in our favor when we remembered land Dave had purchased years before at a tax auction. An unexpected option lay before us: Should we move the home to our land outside of town? We had been working to clear that land, not fully knowing what the plan for it would be. It felt financially irresponsible to move a house to this land we had planned to develop and sell at some point in the future. It also didn't make sense since we already had a home. A home we truly loved. When we built our beloved Victorian-style home in the historic district of Bentonville, Dave and I designed it with the mutual intention of never moving again. We planted maple saplings in anticipation of watching the leaves change from green to red and orange every fall for years to come. We couldn't figure out what we were meant to do with this extravagant gift that felt completely out of place for this season of our lives.

Eventually, we decided to move the house to our land, thinking we could rent it out or use it for retreats or even as a weekend escape for our family. It took about two weeks to prepare the house. Dave poured footings at the new homesite while the house-moving team cut off the original roof. The house was then lifted off the foundation, and the second floor was removed and placed onto a separate flatbed trailer because the home was too tall to pass down the roads at its original height. Each piece of the house was placed onto steel I-beams with wheels added later, to be attached to semi-trucks and driven to the new site.

On a quiet Sunday morning in early December, we woke early in anticipation of the move. I lifted our sleepy toddlers into their car seats, still clad in footie pajamas, and drove to meet Dave at the house, where he had been working since before dawn. The boys and I then drove ahead while Dave's truck followed behind the procession of four semi-trucks carrying various sections of the home. We slowly made our way through town, thankful for the early-morning lack of traffic. Once they arrived at the dirt road leading to the new property, the trucks were unable to make the turn—the house was too wide.

Thankfully, we had met our newest neighbor, Mr. Bob, a few weeks before, and he knew of our plan. He had come outside to see how he could help, and after much discussion and measuring, we decided the best course of action would be to take down his pasture fence and drive the sections of the house through his fifteen-acre field. As the trucks slowly made their way across his property, the soft earth absorbed their weight, and they became lodged. Chains were hooked to bulldozers and tractor-trailer trucks. One at a time, the bulldozers pulled the trucks carrying the house through the pasture. After six hours, the sections had all safely arrived on the new property. The home was perfectly intact: Not a single window was broken and the plaster remained uncracked. An incredible feat. Over the course of the next week, the roof was set back onto the house and the entire structure was placed on its new foundation, overlooking the small pond and future pasture.

We'd spend almost two years designing and restoring the farmhouse, bringing it to life in the limited empty space on our calendars. We threw ourselves into the work, grateful for the distraction from the crushing wait for our daughter. As we removed ceiling tiles in the kitchen, we discovered gorgeous original beams. When we tore up the stained carpeting, we found the original hardwood floors, in need of new stain and polishing. Hidden under shiplap siding, we salvaged a piece of plaster with a Bible verse handwritten in black marker:

Do not fear, for I have redeemed you;
I have summoned you by name; you are mine.

When you pass through the waters,
I will be with you;
and when you pass through the rivers,
they will not sweep over you.
When you walk through the fire,
you will not be burned;
the flames will not set you ablaze.

For I am the Lord your God,
the Holy One of Israel, your Savior ... (Isaiah 43:1-3, NIV)

I saved that piece of plaster as a beautiful fragment of the lives lived in this place before us and as a promise to our own family.

Finding this verse inscribed on the wall felt like a confirmation that this was the home for us. Years before, as Dave and I restored our first house together, I felt called to implement the instructions in Deuteronomy: "These commandments that I give you today are to be on your hearts. . . . Write them on the doorframes of your houses and on your gates" (Deuteronomy 6:6-9, NIV). The Israelites were called to write God's commands on the entryways of their homes to serve as a reminder of God's law as the foundation of their household and family. Over the past decade, Dave and I had been in a recurring cycle of buying a home in need of restoration, renovating it together, and then moving into it for a couple of years before selling it and starting the process again. Each time we started a new restoration project, we took time to pray through each room and ask for discernment over the scripture to record on that room's doorway and walls. We would then write the verses in permanent marker directly on the door trim and the drywall. This had become a beloved, holy tradition that we continue to this day whenever we remodel or build a new space.

During the restoration process, we both fell hard for the quirky old home with all of its odd angles and nooks. Although Dave had originally bought this land without knowing what we would ever do with it, we now knew that this was where we were meant to raise our babies. And so, just as the blossoms of our dogwood tree began to unfurl in the yard, we sold our beloved downtown Victorian in favor of the quiet beckoning of a new life in the country.

I walked through this new-to-us old farmhouse many times, praying for the Holy Spirit to fill this space and for our home to reflect His heart. I prayed for His love and peace to be alive within these walls. I prayed over our children's rooms; I especially prayed my heart out in our daughters' room, asking the Lord to fill both of their little beds. I wrote verses on the walls and doorframes before applying the final coat of paint. On the wall above Sylvie's future bed, I felt led to inscribe: "Look and see, for everyone is coming home! / Your sons are coming from distant lands; / your little daughters will be carried home" (Isaiah 60:4, NLT).

A few weeks after we moved into the farmhouse, boxes still lingered, waiting to be unpacked. The nursery was still in disarray as Dave packed a suitcase and flew over the sea to visit Sylvie. I was thirty-two weeks pregnant with Charlotte and unable to join him because the doctors were concerned about another premature birth and deemed my pregnancy as too high-risk to travel. So the boys and I created care packages for their sister, including hand-drawn cards and photo albums of our family. I wrote a card for Dave to open each day of his trip and sent him with a small journal asking for every moment to be recorded. Even as I was desperate to go, I knew staying home was prudent. I lived in the tension of that season, whispering prayers for Sylvie to come home alongside sincere praise for this new life about to join our family.

Dave's trip had several purposes, but the priority was to get his arms around our daughter to remind her how much she was loved and that we were here fighting, waiting, and praying every moment of every day for her. She was worth every ounce of energy expended calling, emailing, writing letters, and begging anyone and everyone we could think of for help; she was worth every tear and all of this heartache. She is our daughter, and we would never give up fighting to get her home.

When Dave returned, I devoured every word he had written in the little journal. My eyes filled with tears as I read.

I know this week has been hard on you. You have taken over our family at home with no complaint. You allowed me to visit our daughter when I know it just tore at your heart not to be able to be there. But you were there, Jenny. I brought your pictures, your letters, your toys, your love to Sylvie. I told her every day about how very much Mommy and Daddy love her and how we longed to have her home with her brothers. She may not have understood it all, but she knows who we are. She knows her Mommy and Daddy love her so very much and are fighting with everything we have to bring her home.

Six weeks later, at my scheduled checkup, my doctor was concerned with Charlotte's size and the lack of fluid he saw on the ultrasound, so he scheduled a cesarean for the next morning. I remembered the emergency cesarean I'd had with the boys and couldn't help but feel terrified.

Yet, in what I can only describe as a redemptive gift after the traumatizing birth of her brothers, Charlotte's birth was peaceful. The joy in the room was palpable. Dave brought her to me as I lay helplessly on the table, longing to hold her. As if she knew, she looked directly at me with bright, curious eyes that seemed to reflect my own longing. My own eyes welled with tears as I introduced myself to my baby girl. "Hi, Charlotte. I'm your momma. You are the greatest, most surprisingly wonderful gift I've ever been given. I hope you always know how deeply you are loved, my girl."

While I was in recovery, Dave carried Charlotte to the nursery and walked straight to the window, holding her up for the boys and our parents to see. Nathan asked, "Where's the other one?" The concept of just one baby was foreign to him. This is the same little guy who answered "What's your name?" with "NateandBen"—all one word. Ben announced that he would let Charlotte keep his most beloved possessions, including his stuffed "Bailey puppy" for two days and then his "Mr. Bear" for five days. This was true love in the form of a three-year-old brother. I snapped a photo of the boys holding baby Charlotte and sent it to Dr. Laure. She replied immediately, "Jen, you cannot imagine! Sylvie kisses Charlotte, and she's happy and laughing!"

The joy was real at home, yet the ever-present ache was also real. We shifted Sylvie's clothes over in the closet to make room for Charlotte's newborn gear. We boxed up many of the adorable outfits we had for Sylvie, since she had already outgrown them. While it was incredible that we had another little girl to wear these clothes someday, it didn't make my heart hurt any less for all that we had missed with our oldest daughter.

As we settled into a new routine, I cherished the quiet moments with Charlotte. Compared to the chaos of twin preemie newborns, this newborn season felt so natural and calm. I didn't feel rushed to nurse her in order to feed another newborn. I didn't feel torn between holding two crying babies. I simply sat and marveled at how perfect she was. I offered prayers of gratitude for these blessings God had faithfully given and savored this season with my three little loves, while waiting in hopeful anticipation of the day all four little ones would be home together.

CHAPTER 11

HE CARRIED ME HOME

I woke up on an ordinary April morning in 2014 and did the same thing I had done every day for as long as I could remember: I checked my email, looking for word from the embassy or from Dr. Laure in the Congo. No emails with news pertinent to our daughter had arrived, but I noticed an email from a friend who was also waiting for her daughter. She was asking for advice on how to hold on to hope during this wait.

That simple question did it. I suddenly realized I was not keeping it together. Instead, what I was doing was letting go of hope. Over the past week or so, I had let go of believing that the latest news could mean our daughter would come home soon. Three weeks earlier, we received news that children with medical visas could potentially be allowed to receive an exit permit. I was so hopeful, so sure that this was it that I started planning logistics for her homecoming. And then, nothing. No news. No updates. Just waiting . . . in silence. So I started giving up.

Five hundred and seven days had passed since that blustery November day when I first saw Sylvie's face. Two birthdays were celebrated across the sea. Her photo remained on my bathroom mirror, her big, beautiful brown eyes greeting me every morning. Five hundred and seven days of desperate prayers—pleading, begging, facedown-on-the-floor prayers. Five hundred and seven days of imagining what life would look like with her here. Envisioning her in my arms. Five hundred and seven sleepless nights, the persistent ache of her absence palpable in our home.

I hadn't realized I had traveled down this road, slowly inching my way toward despair, until that question was asked. I answered my friend honestly and told her that I was starting to give up and let go of hope, and that was the only way I could make it through the day. That was the only way I could walk into Sylvie's room and not crumble. The only way I could manage to look at her clothes hanging in the closet, her bag packed, or her photos on the wall without weeping.

After letting all of this out, I realized I needed to go ahead and have a talk with Him. God knows my heart. So, I just stopped evading Him and finally admitted what I was doing. I asked forgiveness and asked Him to sustain me once again. I felt a nudge to read over my prayer journal. Paging through, I cried out to Him. *Why? Why, God? Why have you answered almost all of these requests, but my daughter still waits? Why are you ignoring this one? This is important, God. You asked us to walk this road. You brought her into our lives and our hearts. Why would you turn away now?*

A gentle stirring in response: *Read your words again.* I looked through the pages of prayers—miraculous healings, babies coming home, healthy babies born, provision, safety—answered. Then, I saw this verse written in the margin:

The Lord replied,

"Look around at the nations;
Look and be amazed!
For I am doing something in your own day,

something you wouldn't believe

even if someone told you about it." (Habakkuk 1:5, NLT)

At that moment, I felt a deep and peaceful assurance. I knew I could trust that He was at work.

Each day for the next three months, I continued my advocacy efforts. I continued to work with our state representatives in Arkansas and in Washington, D.C. Because Sylvie already held an approved medical visa, we had met with the ambassador at the U.S. Embassy in Kinshasa multiple times to request his help in acquiring a medical exit permit. In early June, he finally agreed to present our documents to the Congolese officials.

We rushed to schedule new medical checkups for Sylvie and request additional letters from specialists. We had the reports translated and submitted to the immigration authorities at the Direction Générale de Migration (DGM), who agreed to review our case. We were cautiously hopeful and mentally prepared to be rejected. They reviewed the documents and asked for our dossier to be submitted immediately. Our agency liaison held all of our documents and refused to turn them over until we paid our final agency fee, which would have normally been paid when we traveled to bring her home. The wiring process would stall us for several days. After much back-and-forth and many tears on my end, our agency agreed to release the documents once we provided proof of the transfer. The documents were mercifully released to Dr. Laure, who submitted the file on our behalf.

Weeks passed without news. I found myself walking in a fog. I hardly slept. I clung to my phone, praying that it would ring or an email update would come through. Instead, I was repeatedly met with silence. My heart grew so very weary.

Then, after the deafening silence, we received news: DGM would review our file on Saturday, July 5. I was a nervous wreck. Our daughter's future depended on the outcome of this review. A text came through early that morning, which was early afternoon in Kinshasa. It was from an adoptive mom friend looking for Laure. "She is there at the office!" I frantically responded, feeling helpless half a world away. My friend couldn't find Laure anywhere.

As I waited for a response, I realized that our beloved dog, Bailey, had not come back in after I let him out earlier. I strapped Charlotte into the carrier and ran outside, searching for him. At twelve years old, he was hard of hearing, but this was unusual behavior, and I worriedly texted all our neighbors. Eventually, one of them found him, injured. He had been hit by a car on our rural dirt road. We rushed to the emergency vet. I sobbed on the short drive over. Right as the vet came out to tell me about the severity of his condition and that I needed to decide about putting him down, my phone rang with a Kinshasa phone number. My hands shook as I answered. Laure gave me the news. "She was approved. She is coming home!"

I was in disbelief. I looked at the vet waiting for my decision regarding Bailey. Tears streamed down my face. I asked Laure if she had the letter in hand and she said no. She was told it would be ready to pick up on Monday. I felt ill. I knew all too well that things could change in two days. This letter could go "missing," and we had no guarantee that she was really coming home.

I hung up, took a deep breath, and focused on saying goodbye to my faithful friend of over a decade. I was heartbroken as I held Bailey and thanked him for being such a good dog. He was my sweet Bailey Bear. My first boy. I would love him and miss him always. As I said goodbye, tears freely fell, and Bailey locked eyes with me in the wise way he had always done. It was as though he were telling me he loved me too and that I'd be okay without him.

The drive home from the vet was somber. I was grief-stricken and I didn't really believe that Sylvie would come home. False hopes and false promises had been such a regular occurrence throughout this journey.

When I arrived home, I put Charlotte down for a nap, and I sent another urgent request asking that Laure be given permission to escort Sylvie home, as we were waiting on Dave's visa. I knew the request was a long shot. I was emotionally exhausted and collapsed into bed that night.

Forty-eight hours later, on Monday, July 7, 2014, I woke up at 4:18 A.M. to the most incredible email from the State Department:

> *Dear Marrs family,*
>
> *We are very happy to inform you that the DGM has told us that Sylvie's exit permit will be ready for pick-up today at noon. Please let us know if you plan on picking it up yourselves while you are in country or whether your in-country representative will be picking it up.*
>
> *Thanks, Saskia*

I ran to the kitchen, where Dave was sipping coffee at the table, and showed him the email. I fell to the floor, tears flowing. I kept repeating, "It's over! It's over!" We had written proof. She was coming home.

I called Laure and found out that she was back at the DGM office picking up Sylvie's exit permit along with her own. She told me that she was given permission to escort Sylvie home. I was shocked and immensely grateful.

We quickly booked flights for Laure and Sylvie. They would leave the next day. This would be the first plane ride for both Laure and Sylvie and they had only twenty-four hours to prepare. My heart was elated and hurting. I was acutely aware that Sylvie would board the plane and leave behind everything and everyone she had ever known. Her world was going to forever change.

The day of Sylvie's arrival felt like a dream. Our nerves were high, and our excitement was palpable. Our incredible community stepped in to help us prepare by bringing groceries, a car seat, clothes, shoes, toys, hair products for Sylvie, and freezer meals. Even though we had waited more than two years for this day, we had only forty-eight hours' notice that she would finally be coming home to us. Those seemingly simple deliveries were immense acts of love for which we will forever be grateful.

Our small airport allowed us to receive special passes to meet the plane at the gate. I couldn't bear another second without holding my girl. In my prayers leading up to this moment, I had asked God to let Sylvie be asleep when the plane landed. Because while this was a day I had desperately prayed for, I was keenly aware that, although we had talked through this journey on FaceTime calls and Dr. Laure had prepared her as best as she could, Sylvie couldn't possibly grasp all that was happening. She was only two and a half years old, and she would undoubtedly be exhausted and most likely confused and afraid. If she was asleep, I could hold her without raising the further fear that I was taking her away from Laure (who would be staying with us in our home to help make the transition smoother). It seemed like a silly prayer in light of all that had transpired, but I had to ask.

And then, just like that, the plane touched down. Six hundred and two days of waiting. Over.

Laure exited the plane with Sylvie sound asleep in the carrier she wore on her back. I ran up to her and hugged her, hoping she could somehow feel my immense love from that simple gesture. I lifted Sylvie from the carrier, in awe of how she remained fast asleep as I did so. God was in every single detail. I walked a few steps to get out of the way of other passengers and then was unable to walk any farther. I sank to the ground in deep, deep relief. I held her tightly as joyful tears streamed down my face. I believe the exhale that took place when she was placed in my arms on U.S. soil was echoed in heaven. The spiritual battle that I couldn't see during those long days and nights was finally over. A celebratory spirit filled the airport arrivals terminal. To this day, whenever I pass gate A6, I say a prayer of gratitude.

During our adoption process, God had led me to Isaiah 60:4, "Look and see, for everyone is coming home! / Your sons are coming from distant lands; / your little daughters will be carried home." I had clung to the verse with a relentless and stubborn hope. Even still, I never expected our daughter to literally be carried home to us by her beloved foster momma and our dear friend. It was more than I could have asked for.

Sylvie's first night home was a whirlwind of laughter and joy and photo-taking. I'll never forget her first bath. I filled our bathtub with warm water and bubbles and gently lifted my daughter up and into the tub. She let out a bloodcurdling scream and pulled her feet up toward her tummy as she neared the water. I looked at Dave in confusion. We tried to talk in soothing tones, failing to calm her hysteria.

Laure, who was staying with us for a week, ran into the small bathroom and translated for us. "C'est bon. Tu es en sécurité." *It's okay. You're safe.* We would recite this phrase hundreds of times over the coming weeks and months.

We learned Sylvie had never been submerged in a bath, she had only stood in a small bucket while a cup filled with cold water was poured over her body. Running water was uncommon, and hot water was a luxury. Mercifully, her tears slowed as Laure explained the water and the bath. Again, I attempted to place her in the tub. She stood inside, staring at us with wide eyes. She reached her little hand out to touch the warm water flowing from the tap, and a delighted smile appeared. She giggled and splashed the water tentatively. I asked Laure to explain that she could sit in the tub, but this was too much to ask so soon. She preferred standing.

Later that night, with her eight-week-old sister asleep nearby in the crib originally intended for her, I snapped a photo as Sylvie giggled on the very first bed she could call her own. Now, finally, the in-between was over. We were here, together. On the frame of the photo were the words inscribed on the wall above the headboard: "*You are so loved.*"

One evening, a year after Sylvie arrived home, a friend was over for dinner and casually mentioned her affinity for the broken spindle on our staircase. She was right: the fourth spindle from the left wobbled and turned. I saw yet another repair. But my friend pointed out how that spindle, in its brokenness, represented more. It continued to hold steadfast to its anchoring nail regardless of the tugging and twirling of little hands seeking amusement, and it served as a reminder to guests that our one-hundred-year-old home was a place where we welcome imperfect people into an imperfect space.

It made me think about how for several years, our family had been caught in the storm. The pulling and tugging of my soul often left me weary and depleted. The battle my family unknowingly stepped into when we said yes to an abandoned little girl across the sea left us all bruised and battered. Yet, God's promises remained steadfast. Even when we lost sight of hope and stumbled toward despair, He was there. Holding on.

Just like that nail at the bottom of the spindle.

Our brokenness remained anchored securely in Him. He faithfully remained regardless of the yanking and demanding of our own hands, begging to be released from the pain of the desert march.

Torn from every familiar thing and placed into our family, my daughter experienced persistent grief and debilitating fear on the day she landed in America. That day, the one I had desperately waited for, for 602 seemingly endless days, was mistakenly seen by outsiders as exclusively celebratory. I cringe at the headlines, scarcely able to skim the surface of her raw, tender identity. AN ORPHAN NO LONGER! A "RESCUED" CHILD! A FAMILY REUNITED!

Although her circumstances were bleak in her home country, it was all she had known. Her first two years of life were marked by survival instincts, extreme hunger, and abandonment. Yet the terror of new people, new sounds, new smells, new food, and a new language was vivid in those early months under our roof. While the battle to get her home was grueling, the real spiritual war had just begun. As a family, we willingly stepped into her brokenness and committed to remain steadfast as we faced the darkness together. We firmly believed that redemption was coming, and restoration was at hand.

I continued to pray, "Jesus, be near." And I continued to marvel at His sufficient grace doled out each day. God's love poured through us and allowed us to hold on even when our home felt like a trauma ward. Even when the brokenness threatened to overwhelm, we could stand firm on His promises of redemption and restoration.

Three hundred and sixty-five days after she landed on U.S. soil, as we lay side by side singing "Jesus Loves Me" before bedtime, Sylvie turned to me and shared a profound truth in her soft, raspy little voice. She whispered in the dark, "God never left me, Momma. He carried me home."

My breath caught in my throat, and I whispered back, "Oh, baby girl. He will never leave. He will always hold on." *Just like the persistent nail at the bottom of that broken spindle,* I thought.

Later that night, after the littles had gone to bed, all was quiet. I stood in my kitchen, glanced around at the scattered toys, the dust bunnies in the corner, the paint chips left by flying Matchbox cars, and that broken old spindle, and breathed in immense gratitude. I'm ever grateful for the joy intermingled with sorrow, the laughter echoing in our four walls after an intense season of pain, and the strength of love forged through brokenness and refined by fire.

CHAPTER 12

WHERE HE LEADS

Two years after Sylvie came home, Dave and I prayerfully made a decision to travel with the kids to South Africa. I would go on to Zimbabwe for five days with two fellow adoptive moms and a nonprofit organization we had worked with for several years. This trip was about being obedient when God calls. As much as I wanted to ignore the call and stay home where it was safe and comfortable, I knew God was leading me over the sea and I had to go. Our kids, ages ranging from two to six, would also have an opportunity to be involved with our nonprofit partners in South Africa, and we would have a chance, as a family, to step away from the breakneck pace of our lives in America for a much-needed respite.

If I'm honest, those first years after Sylvie came home, while Charlotte was an infant and Ben and Nate were rambunctious preschoolers, we were in full-blown survival mode. We were thrown into this family thing in an instant. Yet slowly, one day at a time, the sharp edges of grief and trauma began to soften. The bewildered feelings—not knowing how to parent this hurting little person—started to dissipate. We got to know one another. We started to breathe. In the day-to-day craziness, I often missed the beauty. It got lost somewhere between the sibling squabbles, the piles of laundry, the wet towels and swimsuits, and the endless snacks. But it was there. Just a bit below the surface. A well-earned, hard-fought, relentless beauty.

As we prepared for the trip to South Africa, I was keenly aware of God inviting us into a season of restoration, asking us to lay down the burden of the past decade. I began to see this trip as a very specific opportunity for healing. A time to redeem what had been stolen from my daughter and our family. I hoped that seeing a new place on the same continent as her birth country would add to Sylvie's and my memories of Africa. Memories that would include our entire family together, witnessing beauty, and experiencing peacefulness and wholeness.

The week before we left, God gave me two distinct visions. The first was of a starting line, with our family at the beginning of a freshly paved path. In the other, I could see our family standing together with heavy bags on our backs and shoulders. Slowly, we each heaved the bags to the floor. While doing so, we exhaled deeply and audibly.

On the long flight to South Africa, I processed all that had transpired since first visiting the Congo four years before. Several months after we had returned from that initial trip, we received photos from Dr. Laure after one of her regular visits to the orphanage. One photo stood out to me: a young girl with hollow eyes and a distended belly, the same young girl who had clung to me that day in the orphanage—Harper. The child I had held in my arms just months before was starving to death. I had to do something.

That first step felt so small, foolishly insignificant. Yet, I had to try. I had to get food to Harper and the other children living there. I prayed about a fundraiser. I prayed that God would use it to bring full tummies to the fifty-four children at the orphanage. I didn't know how much we could raise. I just wanted to do something, even if it felt like a tiny drop in the vast sea of need. So I called a few other adoptive moms, and we hosted an online fundraiser, raffling off handmade items we had purchased in the Congo.

God took this tiny drop and turned it into an outpouring of provision. What began as an effort to raise a few hundred dollars resulted in several thousand dollars. We provided two months' worth of food for 151 children living in three orphanages throughout the capital city. When Laure first entered the gates and delivered the food, the children called out in Lingala, "MAMAN AYE NZALA ESILI!" which loosely translates as, *Mom is here, our hunger is finished!*

Within weeks of that first food delivery, Dave and I found ourselves sharing coffee with a young Congolese man attending graduate school at Ozark Christian College in Joplin, Missouri, just one hour from our home in Bentonville. We listened as Tresor Yenyi shared stories of his idyllic childhood in eastern DRC prior to the war. As an adult, he was able to visit the village of his youth, and he saw the devastation of extreme violence firsthand. He listened as women who had been brutally attacked shared their stories of violence and loss. He met young boys who had been taken from their families, forced to become child soldiers and commit atrocious crimes. Tresor went on to create a nonprofit organization, Mwangaza International, devoted to giving victims of war in the Democratic Republic of the Congo a chance at a full life—physically, emotionally, and spiritually.

Over that cup of coffee, Tresor committed to helping our effort to provide a desperately needed stable source of food to that small orphanage in his home country. He and his trustworthy team in Kinshasa partnered with Dave and me to formally establish a nonprofit that we would call "Feed Their Tummies."

Feed Their Tummies was founded as a step forward into the unknown. That first delivery was simply a response to an urgent need for food. Nothing more. It was not strategic, and there were no marketing plans in place or long-term goals established. Yet in that response, God was working. He was revealing His heart—an abundant well of love for His children. We knew God had called us to this place and had introduced us to these precious kids. We knew we could trust Him to provide and it was our job to love them well by meeting their urgent, tangible needs. *Trust God, love people.*

When doubt crept in that first year, as we wondered how we would sustain the funding for this program long-term, God revealed His desire for Dave and me to keep stepping forward when I received a phone call from a friend of a friend, JD Byrum. JD explained that he was preparing to launch a concert series in our town, that they were looking for a nonprofit to which to donate the money generated by the concerts, and asked if Feed Their Tummies would accept the proceeds. We were in awe of how God used the generosity of our neighbors to help us fund this work overseas. In large part because of that little concert series, named "The Bentonville Sessions," we began feeding nearly two hundred children three nutritious meals every single day through Tresor's team.

In 2015, we started conversations with another trusted nonprofit organization we had been financially supporting for many years, Help One Now, about partnering in the Congo. Dave, JD, Tresor, and Lamar, the international director for Help One Now, decided to take a trip to the capital city of Kinshasa to meet with Tresor's team on the ground. The goal of this trip was twofold: to discern how to care well for the vulnerable where our feeding program was established and, most important, to learn how best to empower the local leaders we worked with to transform their communities long-term. As much as I wanted to go, we decided it would be wise for me to stay home to keep stability in our schedule for Sylvie, who still very much needed the predictability of a consistent routine. My still-newly-home toddler needed me, and following God's lead is not always an adventure—sometimes it's a sacrificial way of living that allows Him to work amidst very ordinary circumstances.

On the way home from the Congo, Dave and the team stopped in South Africa to meet with locals who were doing the work of caring for the vulnerable in their community. He stayed with a family of four, the de Jagers, who hosted him with the most gracious and warm hospitality. He enjoyed the luxury of a hot shower, delicious food, and good company. Next, he would stop for a few days in a rural village in Zimbabwe to meet with Help One Now's leaders in that community: Pastor John Chinyowa and his wife, Orpah. John and Orpah were the first leaders Help One Now had partnered with nearly seven years before. They were also the leaders our family had been supporting monthly all that time. Dave had assumed Zimbabwe would be much like the Congo, and, in his exhaustion, he was just ready to be back home. Yet he also knew it was important to stop there to learn from John and Orpah's work and find out how we could apply the work to the Congolese initiatives.

Dave called me as soon as he arrived at their home to share how incredibly warm and welcoming they were. He was struck by the joy and hope he felt in Zimbabwe. He was immensely impressed as he toured the children's home they had founded and learned more about their work. Pastor John took Dave to see a farm he hoped to purchase someday to feed the children and teach them how to farm. When Dave called, relaying the details of the day, the excitement in his voice was palpable. He knew there was something special about that patch of farmland in Zimbabwe and that God had brought him there for a purpose.

After Dave returned, unbeknownst to us, the seeds were sown that would further our connection to that farm across the sea. Seemingly out of nowhere, a neighbor called, offering us an amazing price for twenty acres of land near our farmhouse. We prayed and purchased this new plot as an act of obedience, trusting that God was at work. God led every step of the way. He gave us an idea for the land: a blueberry farm. We had no experience in farming and knew nothing about growing blueberries. So He brought an agricultural expert into our lives as a great friend and mentor.

When Dave first mentioned the idea, I asked, "Why blueberries?"

I half-expected a simple answer about how we loved the fruit. Instead he responded, "Blueberries will yield fruit over a long period of time. If we nurture them and properly care for them, the investment will span decades. It's like how we are investing in the lives of the children in our program—we aren't looking to solve long-standing issues of hunger and poverty with a short-term investment. We're committed to the long haul with these kids."

We determined that the land would become the Feed Their Tummies Blueberry Farm. The fruit would generate profits to feed our program's vulnerable, orphaned, and abandoned children. We felt called to care for these kids and we would move forward in our small role, desiring restoration and hope for each child.

After working for months to prepare the fields and install irrigation lines, our family and a handful of close friends spent several days in 2015 planting 1,500 blueberry plants in anticipation of the future harvest, knowing it would take several years for the plants to produce fruit. At the same time, we learned the community center work we'd hoped to initiate in the Congo had to be halted due to further political instability in the country. We were at a crossroads, and, if I'm honest, I was feeling untethered and confused. I couldn't understand why God had brought us this far, why He had allowed the partnership with Help One Now and sent Dave and a team back to the Congo to plan for the next phase of development work, only to have it all stop now.

God was silent, and I was angry. We had poured so much into this work. I remember walking the fields as a family every evening after dinner for months and months, praying over the soil and the land. We prayed for God to use the space for His glory. During those prayer walks, I became aware of the call to create a gathering place. I prayed for God to draw people there. Yet I had no idea how the land would be used now that the program we had worked so hard to establish seemed to be deteriorating in an instant.

In that season, the political and economic situation in the Congo became more and more unstable. Our dear friend Tresor advised us to continue the work of caring for the vulnerable but to do so elsewhere. Again, I was confused. How could I abandon these children and this place we so dearly loved? Again, God provided. We were able to secure donors for monthly sponsorships for each of the children in the program. Tresor assured us that his organization would continue to do the work there.

One afternoon, as I drove to pick up the kids from school, I felt an undeniable urge to travel to Zimbabwe to join a team from Help One Now. I called Dave immediately and shared the idea with him. I had no idea why or what the trip would look like, but I knew I needed to go. I needed to visit the place that had captured Dave's heart and meet Pastor John, the man who had gained his respect. We both knew this was the beginning of something, yet neither of us had any idea what was in store.

We found ourselves in another season of uncertainty, but we knew we simply needed to do the one thing right in front of us, take the one step forward in faith. For me, right then, that one thing involved conquering a very real fear and boarding an airplane, this time on my own, to Zimbabwe. That was all. I just had to get on the plane.

CHAPTER 13

OBEDIENCE BRINGS BLESSINGS AND LIFE

he night before I boarded the flight to Zimbabwe, leaving Dave and my four small children in South Africa, I woke up at midnight, gripped with fear. I couldn't shake my worries and found myself texting a few close friends who were back home praying for our family. As I prayed and friends on the other side of the ocean prayed with me, I felt peace settle my anxiety.

The flip side of the beauty of travel, the half I can't ignore or pretend doesn't exist for me, is fear. The first time I distinctly remember being terrified on a plane was when I was twenty-five years old. I was flying to Sacramento for a quick work trip. As I fastened my seat belt and heard the familiar words spoken by the flight attendant pointing out the safety exits, the elderly woman who sat beside me leaned over and asked how often I fly. When I explained that I fly quite often, she shared that she was anxious and hadn't traveled by plane in many years. I calmly assured her we were safe and that everything would be fine.

About thirty minutes into the flight, a large flame erupted outside my window. At the same time, the interior cabin lights went dark. I remember seeing a flight attendant run past me, visibly distressed. My legs began trembling and my heart raced. I knew something was wrong. When the captain's voice came over the speaker, he announced in a solemn yet steady tone that we had lost an engine and would be making an emergency landing at the nearest airport, in Houston, Texas.

The flight attendants shouted instructions to cross our arms, grip the seat in front of us, and duck our heads. I heard the man across the aisle explain that the engine fire, combined with possible leaking gas, could be catastrophic upon landing. I could hear the repeated shouts from the flight attendants: "BRACE!" "BRACE!" "BRACE!" The words felt as though they were being seared into my brain. As we approached the airport, dusk had settled, and I could make out the flashing lights of dozens of emergency vehicles lining the runway, awaiting our approach.

Instead of grasping the seat in front of me with both hands, I tightly gripped the time-weathered hand beside me. The kind elderly lady held fast as we both recited the Lord's Prayer. It was the prayer of my childhood. I had repeated the words thousands of times before. Now they served as a lifeline.

> *Our Father, who art in heaven, hallowed be thy name.*
> *Thy kingdom come.*
> *Thy will be done, on earth as it is in heaven.*
> *Give us this day our daily bread.*
> *And forgive us our trespasses as we forgive those who*
> *trespass against us.*
> *And lead us not into temptation, but deliver us from*
> *evil,*
> *For thine is the kingdom, and the power, and the glory,*
> *forever and ever.*
> *Amen.*

No other words would come. Only these ancient words, a prayer Jesus used to teach us how to pray. We repeated them. My breath catching with each syllable. My heart thundering in my chest. My voice trembling within the stronghold of fear. As we prayed, the plane descended. Slowly.

BRACE! BRACE! BRACE!

The flight attendant's instructions came louder and faster. We were approaching the runway, and my fellow passengers were screaming. There was hysteria and terror inside that airplane. Yet everything moved slowly; it felt as though this older woman and I were suspended in time.

Our Father, who art in heaven, hallowed be thy name.

BRACE! BRACE! BRACE!

I clung to her hand. Tears freely fell. We closed in on the runway. The sirens and flashing lights in clear view.

The familiar thud of wheels touching down. Skidding brakes. Breath held.

A moment of complete quiet. Then, chaos erupted. Passengers were shouting and scrambling to exit. Everyone feared the plane might catch fire. No fire came. We were safe. The flight attendants announced we would be towed in to a gate and instructed everyone to get back to their seats. After the doors finally opened, we all gathered our belongings and exited the plane. I lost track of the woman in the hurried exit. I never learned her name and never saw her again. To this day, I believe God placed her in that seat beside me. She held my hand on behalf of His.

After that flight, I had to board another one to get to Sacramento. I was terrified. I wanted to rent a car and drive the nine hours home. Instead, I boarded a second plane. I went on the trip, and then I did it again the next month and the next and the next. For the next six years, I traveled frequently for work. Often I was scared. More often I was okay. In the years since, I still travel for work, and I also travel with my family on adventures, and since I've had kids, the unsettling fear creeps in more often than not.

So, I'm afraid to fly. It's immensely frustrating. And mostly, it's something I never, ever want to pass on to my kids. This is why I force myself to get on the plane even when my legs are quite literally shaking, my palms are sweating, and my breathing is shallow. I refuse to believe that my faith is in any way diminished by my fear. I refuse to listen to anyone who tells me that I am not trusting in God in those moments. Because of my faith, because of my deep, deep trust in my faithful God, I bought the plane ticket in the first place. Because of my faith, because of my trust, I walk onto the plane and latch my seat belt.

Often, as the plane begins to ascend, I recite an abridged version of Deuteronomy 7:18–19: "Don't be afraid. *Remember, remember, remember.*" I lean into Moses's antidote for fear by focusing on remembering all the flights I've taken in the past and all the times God has been faithful during those flights.

For I know that when I'm flying through the air, trapped in a metal tube, with zero control over my circumstances, I depend wholly and completely on Him. I cling to Jesus in those moments. I cry out to Him in desperation, and He meets me with peace and assurance and reminders of His past faithfulness. In my everyday life, I don't often ache for Him. I run from commitment to commitment. I meet pressing deadlines. I answer the constant onslaught of communication via text and email. I worry over details. I forget to rest.

Maybe this is why He set within me a yearning for adventure. Maybe this is why He keeps leading me to faraway lands only accessible by an airplane. For it's in that plane—the place where I'm most uncomfortable and afraid, where I feel most frail and incapable—that I am most acutely aware of His presence. And, in the way that only God can, He uses all things for my good and His glory. He redeems my moments of fear and meager offerings of faith to remind me that He is near. That He is faithful. That I can trust Him.

Before leaving for the airport to board my flight to Zimbabwe, I opened my Bible and was led to Deuteronomy: "If you obey all the decrees and commands I am giving you today, all will be well with you and your children" (Deuteronomy 4:40, NLT). It wasn't until I read the note I had written in the margins that I realized what God was showing me. *Obedience brings blessings and life.*

God knows me. He knows the last place I want to be is flying in an airplane, away from my family. So, with five words, He reminded me that going to this unknown place for an unknown purpose was an act of obedience.

I was a blubbering mess when Dave and the kids dropped me off at the airport. My sweet Ben looked at me and said, "Momma, I'm proud of you." That did it. I was undone and filled up at the same moment. Teary goodbyes were said, and multiple hugs were given as I slowly made my way into the airport. I checked in and found myself standing at the entrance to the security line, unable to step forward. I was paralyzed with fear. I wanted to turn around and run back to my family. Images from my time in the Congo replayed in my mind. As much as I loved the country and the people, my experiences there had been extremely painful, and I feared my time in Zimbabwe would be similar.

Eventually, I boarded my flight, and when I landed and walked into the airport in Zimbabwe, there were no machine guns or shouting. There was no chaos. Instead calm, orderly lines were formed as people waited to receive entrance visas. The customs officer joked with me as he stamped my passport. Armed guards weren't at the exit, searching through my bag only to take whatever items suited them. I simply exited the airport peacefully. God whispered to my heart, *See. It's going to be different this time.*

I looked up and saw Pastor John Chinyowa. He was standing there, arms spread wide, a smile across his beaming face. As I walked into his embrace, I felt absolute peace and a rekindling of hope.

We drove to lunch and then on to John and Orpah's cozy and inviting home. I was struck by the lushness of the land, the vivid green grass and trees, and the bright blue of the clear sky. After arriving, we walked to the end of the road to see the sunset. By this time, dark clouds had rolled in, covering the glow of the setting sun, but not even dark clouds could conceal the awe-inspiring beauty before us.

The morning after the group I was traveling with arrived, we visited the children's home served by Pastor John, Orpah, and their local church. The children's needs were great, yet the community caring for the eighty orphans made up for the lack of resources with selfless and generous love. What stood out to me most were the children's bright eyes—they held life, hope, and laughter despite their circumstances.

I spent the better part of one day listening to each child share his or her dreams with me as I recorded video footage to be shown to new sponsors and at our Bentonville Sessions shows. I heard from future pilots and teachers and doctors and nurses and a lawyer and a judge and a psychologist and a boy with a wide smile who captured my heart—a future pastor who had been nicknamed Pastor by his friends. These children were not without hope; they had ambitious goals for their futures—which was a huge testament to the good work being done in this place.

We had the awesome privilege of attending Pastor John's church that Sunday. I can say without reservation that it was the most powerful, pure, and holy worship I have ever experienced. Members of the congregation prayed and sang as the Spirit led. At one point, one of the members of the church, Dr. Ferrerai, recounted hardships they had endured as a community and as a nation, and then he turned it all into praise. The community praised God for their blessings despite their hardships and sufferings, singing "Blessed Be the Name of the Lord" in harmonious response.

We visited the farmland Pastor John had shown Dave the year before. Afterward, we sat around his table as he shared his dreams for the land over a delicious meal. We learned about the orphaned and abandoned teen boys in the children's home and the fact that they would be back on the streets at eighteen without an education or a skill. The cycle of extreme poverty needed to be broken, and Pastor John believed that it could begin with these boys. He dreamed of a farm on that land where the boys could learn the lost skill of caring for the soil. An idea sparked: *Our farm at home could fund this farm here.*

I left with such a strong sense of hope, purpose, and determination. I knew God had brought Dave to this place for a purpose. And He had done the same for me. I left with renewed enthusiasm to go home and work hard advocating for these precious children. I didn't know all that God would have in store for our family in connection with this beautiful land and these warmhearted people, yet I knew something good was in the works. God went before us many years ago, preparing us for this work. Our connection to this country and these children originally began seven years before with our first child sponsored through Help One Now. Seeds had been planted in our hearts along the way, tethering us to this country and the African continent in profound ways.

Five months after we returned home from Zimbabwe, in the summer of 2017, the blueberries were ripe and we were ready to announce the launch of The Berry Farm. Two years before, just after we had planted the berries, we were uncertain what would become of the farm when our work in the Congo was halted due to political instability. Despite our limited scope of understanding, we knew God had called us to this work, and we simply continued to focus on the one thing before us and trust God for the rest. We planted the fields, we tended the plants, and we prayed over the land. As our relationship with Pastor John and Orpah grew, God made it clear that He had had a different plan for these fields all along: We were to use the proceeds from our farm to fund the agricultural training school that Pastor John dreamed of.

We woke on the morning of the very first U-pick to find that an overnight storm had destroyed our crop. Frustrated, we canceled the event. A week or so later, we had enough ripe berries to try again. We sent out word to everyone we knew: *This is it! It's time to gather in the fields to pick blueberries!* And the morning of the scheduled U-pick, we checked the fields and found that our crop had already been eaten by birds.

That first year was tough. Our commitment to Pastor

John in Zimbabwe was $50,000—the cost of launching and fully funding the agricultural training program for the year. We had done the math before the start of the season and felt confident we could fulfill our commitment. Because of the struggle with the storm and the birds, we made only $8,000 that first year. We felt defeated. We knew we had heard God correctly, but things were not turning out as we had planned.

At the end of that first harvest, we had no way of knowing that over the next seven years, we would gather thousands of families at our farm each summer to pick blueberries. We had no way of knowing that the dream of one man in Zimbabwe would be realized thanks to this little plot of land in the northwest corner of Arkansas. We had no way of knowing that Pastor John would successfully launch the trade school in Zimbabwe, dorms would be built on the campus, and countless lives would be changed. We had no way of knowing that we would welcome Pastor John and Orpah to our farm to walk and pray in the fields alongside us. We had no way of knowing that the little boy who had captured my heart, the one lovingly nicknamed Pastor, would go on to graduate from that trade school across the sea. We had no way of knowing that we would partner with our local children's shelter and serve foster families in our community on this land. We had no way of knowing that weddings would be celebrated and new lives would be embarked upon on this very special soil. We simply obeyed, even when it made absolutely no sense. Obedience brings blessings and life, indeed.

CHAPTER 14

◦◇◦

GO WITH THE
STRENGTH YOU HAVE

After my time in Zimbabwe, I flew back to South Africa to join Dave and the kids for a few weeks of exploring together. The last leg of our trip was full of breathtaking natural beauty and deep soul rest. We went on safari and the boys surfed in the Indian Ocean while the girls and I cheered from the sandy shore. We sunbathed alongside penguins on Boulders Beach and laughed when a monkey squeezed through the window of our rental house and stole a banana from our kitchen countertop. The time away together was marked by beautiful words like "intentionality," "laughter," "calm," "contentment," and "joy." Healing began, connections deepened, and quiet moments ushered in a slower, less frazzled pace.

One morning, we were sipping coffee on the patio of our vacation rental in the coastal town of Ballito when we received a phone call from a production company sharing the news that HGTV was interested in filming a sizzle reel for a possible television show featuring our work renovating historic homes in our town. About six months prior, an executive at the network had visited Bentonville and, enamored with the small-town charm, had asked around for recommendations of married couples who restored homes. When we first received the email asking if we'd be interested in having our lives documented (and confirmed that it was not, in fact, spam), we were adamant in our refusal. However, after all that had transpired in Zimbabwe and with a fresh perspective from our time away, we now saw the show as an opportunity to share the work we cared deeply about, happening both in Africa and back home on our farm. We took several days to pray about it, and eventually Dave and I felt that a television show could be a platform to share about adoption and redemption and caring well for our neighbors—whether down the street or across the sea. We said yes.

Back home, we welcomed Jerome and Carl, two camera operators; Chaz, a sound engineer; Tim, a producer; and Steven, a production assistant, into our home and our lives for two days. They followed us around as we worked and then interviewed us about our family and renovating historic homes. I remember watching the three-minute edited-down sizzle reel that was sent to HGTV and thinking, *This is crazy. Why would anyone want to watch a television show about our lives?* I also remember being extremely nervous that someone *would* want to watch a television show about our lives. At the time, Charlotte was two, Sylvie was four, and Ben and Nate were six. They were babies. Was it wise to open our family up to the inevitable criticism and loss of privacy that must come with a television show? (I may never know the answer to this question. It certainly has been complicated and challenging. Over the years, I have felt the enemy's attacks often, especially around the topic of our transracial adoption, yet I have also known the abundant mercy and protection of my Father. He loves my kids more than I do, and He knew what their childhood would look like. He knew it would be unique and unusual, and He put safeguards in place back when we were first considering this career move that I couldn't fully appreciate at the time—including where we lived, where they went to school, whom we surrounded ourselves with, where we went to church—that I can look back on and see as His merciful hand of protection.)

Two months later, we learned HGTV had given the green light to film a pilot, tentatively named *Almost Home,* which filmed in June and then aired in November. We gathered with friends to watch the episode, laughing together and truly believing this was a one-time thing.

The pilot episode did well enough that the series was picked up for a full season. Reflecting on this, I wrote in my journal:

I feel like we are stepping onto a battlefield spiritually by saying yes to this show. I know how ruthless the enemy is, but I also know that every attack must first come through the hand of God. We are His. He goes before and behind and surrounds us on every side. The enemy has no power over us, and while he may try to quiet us, we will walk forward in faith and keep our eyes fixed on Jesus. May our lives testify His goodness and glory alone. Lord—help us not to be overwhelmed by fear of what may come or the pressure to please man. Prevent pride from gaining a foothold. Keep humility in our hearts. Help us to look to you for our worth, not the words or affirmation or judgment or criticism of others.

We met with our production company and discussed expectations for this show. Dave and I were insistent on one thing: authenticity. We had no way of knowing how other shows worked, but we knew that this was our real life, our real work, and our real family. We weren't interested in pretending or playing or acting. We wanted to ensure everything portrayed on our show was authentic. We all agreed to include the inevitable mistakes, the challenges, and the actual work happening. We didn't want to let others do our jobs and then sweep in and take credit for the work. As the team outlined the schedule, we quickly learned that the demands on our time would be intense. The production schedule for the first season required that we renovate two homes simultaneously within five weeks, consecutively over six months. (In comparison, renovating an entire historic home in "real life" typically takes a full year, often longer.) This proposed schedule would undoubtedly be grueling, and while we had built and remodeled hundreds of homes in our career, we had never done so under so much pressure and under the demanding time constraints of a production calendar.

Filming started and was immediately a whirlwind. After renovating the first two homes of the season, I was exhausted. I felt overwhelmed and unsettled. I couldn't find my footing or any semblance of balance between the production schedule and the needs for the renovations, on top of our normal responsibilities with the kids' schedules and their school needs. Morning routines were chaotic. I felt frenzied, rushed, and always behind. I missed the normalcy of seeing friends in the evenings or arranging my work schedule to allow time for popping into the kids' school to meet them for lunch. I kept telling myself, "We just have to make it through to July," when filming was scheduled to wrap. But I also knew that was no way to live. I didn't want to trudge through entire months of my life, waiting to exhale and longing for some finish line just out of reach.

Originally, we had planned to film eight episodes. Then the network added two more episodes for the season, which extended our filming time. This was exciting news because it meant they liked what they were seeing as the edits came through. We had worked so very hard, and it was reassuring that the network felt we were creating something good. Yet, at the risk of sounding ungrateful, I wasn't thrilled when I first found out about the extension. We were in the middle of filming three episodes and I was desperate for a break. I was burned-out from the long days (and from being away from my kids during their summer vacation), and the news of two more episodes brought me to tears. On top of the exhaustion, I knew I needed a break when I stopped picking up my camera, writing, reading, or doing any of the things that enable the right side of my brain to thrive.

I had a nice long chat with God about all of this and the whole why-did-you-choose-us-for-this thing, and He led me to the book of Judges, of all places. "Go with the strength you have . . ." (Judges 6:14, NLT).

I love the story of Gideon in Judges. Thank you, Jesus, for including all of these flawed humans in your Word. Because if Gideon can tell God that he isn't fit for the task that an angel of the Lord told him about face-to-face, then I certainly can bring my own "Lord, you chose the wrong person" prayers to Him.

He responded to me, in no uncertain terms: *I will be with you. I love you. Shine my light. Go with the strength you have.* Those words made me remember that He'll always use my weakness to display His power. I wrote those exact words down as a reminder, and *Shine His light* became my daily mantra.

God's strength is sufficient even in something as wild as being exhausted from filming a television show. And, most assuredly, His strength was sufficient when I was up all night rocking our traumatized toddler, or when fear clouded my vision 30,000 feet above the ground, or when I was holding starving children in a seemingly forgotten orphanage in the Congo. In every season, no matter how unexpected or seemingly mundane, His strength has always been enough.

CHAPTER 15

GOD WITH US

On the fourteenth of October, one week after we completed filming the first season, I woke up not feeling well. I had an old pregnancy test in the cabinet and had a strange inkling to take it, never in a million years thinking it would be positive. It was. I was shocked. I ran outside to show Dave, who was walking in from the barn. I sat in the driveway in disbelief.

My mind flashed back to that first Father's Day, ten years before, when I wrapped up another little stick with two pink lines as a present for my husband, then father-to-be. We celebrated and cried tears of joy. It had been a long year of uncertainty, and those two lines were a precious gift, the timing astoundingly perfect. When the doctor later explained that I had lost the baby, I was numb.

This new stick confirmed once more that our story wasn't over back then and that loss would not define our family. Throughout our struggle to build our family, I had clung to the Biblical story of Hannah. She, in her deep anguish, had pleaded with God for a baby. When she was pregnant with Samuel, she promised the baby back to God and fulfilled that promise by leaving Samuel as a young boy to serve the Lord as an assistant to the priest, despite how heartbreakingly cruel that must have felt to her momma's heart. Her prayer of praise recorded in 1 Samuel 2 was one I had read and recited repeatedly. Ten years later, a new verse caught my eye for the first time:

Before they returned home, Eli would bless Elkanah and his wife and say, "May the Lord give you other children to take the place of this one she gave to the Lord." And the Lord blessed Hannah, and she conceived and gave birth to *three sons and two daughters.* (1 Samuel 2:20-21, NLT, emphasis added)

I knew at that moment that this new baby on the way would be a boy. *Three sons and two daughters to take the place of the one she gave to the Lord.* It was more than I ever could have hoped for. We decided on the name Luke, which means "light-giving." This baby boy would be the most unexpected yet most absurdly, over-whelmingly good blessing we would ever receive. We thought our family was done growing; we never had this little man on our radar. We were done with diapers and had given away all our "baby things." The timing of his birth felt wild and crazy. I felt too old to start over. Yet he would complete our family in a way we didn't know we needed. Through this new life, God restored my heart, closed the door on a long season of waiting, and ushered me toward a grace-laden season of joy.

After visiting the doctor, who confirmed the baby was healthy and had a strong heartbeat, we came home and showed the kids the ultrasound photo. I asked, "What do you think this is a picture of?" Ben replied quickly, "A baby." I asked him how he knew, and he responded matter-of-factly, "It says so right there," as he pointed to the corner of the photo. Sylvie excitedly asked, "So there's a baby in your tummy?" Nathan thought we were playing a prank, and Charlotte was beside herself with joy. She kissed my belly continuously and made sure I knew she wasn't kissing me, she was kissing the baby. In her sweet four-year-old voice, she looked up and said, "Momma, I really wanted a baby!"

The evening before, Pastor John and Orpah had arrived from Zimbabwe to visit the farm and were quietly listening as we told the kids about the baby. Once the excitement died down, Orpah held her hand on my abdomen and prayed for abundant blessings over this new life. We stood together in my kitchen as she spoke words of truth over our son. More than a year and a half later, she and John would be back in town and again we would stand together in my kitchen, this time with seven-month-old Luke in Orpah's arms.

As we began preparing for his arrival, we knew it was time to renovate the farmhouse once again. We had three bedrooms and would soon have seven humans living under this roof. The boys wanted to stay in their room together, but we decided to move the girls out of their shared room and into individual rooms. They were overjoyed at the idea, and we turned the former playroom into Charlotte's new room and bumped out a dormer to add a room for Sylvie. The girls picked paint colors and helped with the details of their new rooms while I redecorated their former nursery for baby Luke. Before we painted, I inscribed 1 Chronicles 29:14 (NLT) on his wall: "Everything we have comes from you. . . ."

All the while, I had a nagging concern about the long, taxing hours of filming if the show was renewed for another season. How would I manage with a newborn? It seemed impossible. It turned out God had other plans. The first season wouldn't premiere until the next fall.

Then, on June 11, 2019, our world forever changed for the better when the most astounding blessing entered the world. When Dave was able to bring him over to me on the operating table, Luke opened his eyes and looked right at me the instant he heard me say, "Welcome to the world, little man." We locked eyes, and everyone in the room remarked on the way he recognized my voice instantly. It was a sacred moment that I will forever cherish.

We began filming season two when Luke was six months old. It was a gift that I had been able to relish every minute of my pregnancy, as well as the precious, fleeting newborn days with my baby boy. God is ever faithful.

After we started filming again, we fell into a new routine. I would breastfeed Luke in the morning before I left each day and then would pump on construction sites, in Dave's truck, or in bathroom stalls all around town. I'll never forget the time I sat in a half-demo'd room, the door lodged shut (locks had not yet been installed), and sweet Mr. Joe, whom we had worked with for over a decade and who was assisting that day, walked in to find me pumping. I was covered by a blanket, but he panicked and quickly stumbled backward out of the room, apologizing profusely. He wouldn't look me in the eye for weeks afterward.

When Luke was nine months old, on March 17, 2020, I wrote in my journal:

The film crew flew home yesterday. There is a rumor of a mandatory quarantine being announced today. I'm thankful to be home with my family.

Then, on April 7, 2020:

They announced yesterday that school will not go back into session this year. The kids and I sat around the table, voicing our sadness over what they/we will miss. Charlotte said, "So, Ms. Guthrie will never be my teacher again?" with tears in her eyes.

The world had shut down, and our kids were out of school, but we resumed filming and were going to work each morning as though nothing had changed. We would drive on empty roads to the houses we were renovating and pack our lunches because no restaurants were open. I'd come home at the end of each day and shower before

I held my baby and nursed him. Every single day, I prayed the verse God had laid on my heart at the start of the year: "Lord, you are our Mighty One. Please be a wide river of protection that no enemy—no virus—can cross" (Isaiah 33:21).

A full year later, I woke up with a fever. I tested positive for Covid and spent the next two weeks in bed, the sickest I could remember being in a very long time. Thankfully, Dave and the kids stayed healthy, but my parents, who had recently moved to Northwest Arkansas and had been helping us with the kids, both tested positive. After two very long weeks, I was back to work, even if the lingering exhaustion meant I had to nap in the car throughout the day.

A few days after I went back to work, we were standing in front of a home, waiting for the owners to arrive for their reveal, when my phone buzzed in my back pocket. It was my mom. I could barely understand what she was saying; she was hyperventilating and telling me that Dad was unresponsive and the ambulance was on the way. I knew my dad wasn't healing quickly, but this news came as a shock. I composed myself enough to finish the reveal, and then, with blessings and prayers from our entire production team, I raced to the hospital.

When I got to the hospital, I learned how very sick my dad was. Due to the restrictions, we weren't allowed back with him, and he told us later how scared and alone he felt. In the days that followed, the doctor told us he needed to be placed on a ventilator. My mom collapsed when the doctor said the words. Given what we knew at that time, the ventilator felt like a death sentence. Before the procedure, his nurses permitted us to stand outside my dad's hospital room, hands pressed to the glass on the door, while he held a phone, allowing us to talk to him. We stood there, huddled in a semicircle of defiance, and spoke words of life and truth over my brave, yet terrified, daddy. Every nurse and doctor on the floor paused with us and joined in prayer. We were in the battle, and we were not going down without a fight. We texted our friends, family, and co-workers, and a gathering of all the people we love came together in the parking lot of the hospital. My sweet Mr. Joe, who loves my dad dearly, hugged me, and I lost it. We both cried. I just couldn't get over the way all our people showed up to hold my dad in prayer.

I'm no stranger to the in-between. The waiting. The expectant Hope. The held breath. I've walked through enough seasons of uncertainty to know that God remains faithful even when we can't see past our fear and doubt.

We spent weeks outside my dad's hospital window while he fought for life inside. Listening to my babies pray with an equal measure of confidence and desperation was both heart-filling and soul-crushing. I begged God to answer their prayers. We all knew the prayers were asking for a miracle.

A miracle was the only way.

In those weeks, God spoke so clearly through His Word. He would send it to me when I needed it most, through a friend, a verse, or a song. He reminded me over and over: *Do not fear. I am here. I hear your prayers, and I see your tears. I'm at work. Be still and watch. I'm going to do something that will astound you.*

He is ever faithful. He always astounds. He is always near. He shifts the energy in a room from fear and panic to peace and quiet trust.

Within the month, remarkably, my dad improved enough to be weaned off the ventilator and moved into a rehabilitation facility. We received our miracle when he was released to come home just in time for Christmas. In Isaiah, He says, "Do not be afraid, for I am with you" (Isaiah, 43:5, NLT). That's the beauty of the Christmas story, after all. God is with us. Even now, even in this broken and scary world, He is right here. Always, ever faithful.

CHAPTER 16

LESSONS FROM THE FARM

Not long after we had moved out of town to the farmhouse, the long days at home with a newborn, a toddler, and two preschoolers had me wanting a large dog to bark and alert us of any danger on our property. One afternoon, I loaded up the kids and we headed to visit our local animal shelter. There we met Dora, a two-year-old black Lab who was described as "rambunctious" and unsuitable for a home with young kids. We were told that Dora was on her last day and, although we were interested in her, our home would not be compatible because of our young children. She would be euthanized the next day. We stood our ground and refused to leave without her. I called Dave, and he left work to meet us at the shelter. Together, we pleaded with the staff as the boys tossed a ball with Dora in the play enclosure. Eventually, they relented, and we came home with our new pup, who turned out to be just perfect for a family with children.

Dora was the first animal we added to the farm. Over the years, we have taken in dogs, cats, cows, sheep, chickens, a donkey, two llamas, an alpaca, and a horse. Somehow, they each found their way to us. As a result, the lessons I've learned on this farm have marked my life. I could tell a thousand stories about what these animals have taught me about our Good Shepherd.

One afternoon, our sheep farmer neighbor, Mr. Tommy, called to ask if I'd be willing to care for one of his orphaned lambs. Without hesitation, I enthusiastically responded, "Yes!" The kids and I had visited his farm many times to hold newborn lambs and feed the momma sheep, and I had not-so-casually mentioned my affinity for sheep to him during each visit. Dave also knew I would have loved to add sheep to our little hobby farm. At the time, we had chickens and a few cows, but I'd always had a special admiration for the peacefulness and beauty of flocks of sheep grazing in a pasture.

An orphaned lamb requires around-the-clock care; it must be bottle-fed every couple of hours. So I'd forgo sleep, holding our newly named Trixie in my lap while *she* slept. If I tried to place her into the kennel we had set up for her, she would wake instantly and start to cry. Her sad and lonely "baaa" broke my heart, so I'd always give in and hold her. One morning, as I cradled this innocent, fragile little lamb who was wholly dependent on me for sustenance and safety, I read my own journaled words from when we were still fighting to get Sylvie home and was newly struck by their significance.

God will always provide. Strength. Peace. Joy. One moment, one step, one day at a time. Like a Good Shepherd leading his sheep, we can trust He will guide us to green pastures. We can keep our ears tilted toward Him, listening for the next place to place our feet. The next stop. The next fork in the road. Ours is meant to be a position of dependence on Him.

Trixie went on walks with our family and our dogs along the dirt road in the evenings and would come running at the sound of my voice. She'd snuggle up to Dora on the front porch, and I'm fairly certain she thought she was a dog. Eventually, Mr. Tommy had two male lambs in need of bottle-feeding and we took them in as well. As they grew, we built a fence around the front pasture where the three sheep eventually lived and began to understand that they were, in fact, sheep.

Trixie had a baby that spring and then again the next spring, and then her babies had babies, and we had a small flock of our own.

One morning, we woke to find Trixie's daughter, Lola, had delivered twins in the night. The kids named the little one Elmo and his brother Tater Tot. The smaller lamb was lethargic, and as I assessed the baby, I noticed he wasn't eating. I called another set of sheep farmer neighbors, Will and Waltina, who graciously dropped what they were doing and raced over with a box full of supplies to administer a tube feed of nutrient-dense colostrum. We placed Lola and her twins in a private pen within the sheep barn to encourage bonding, knowing the first twenty-four hours were critical. If this new lamb didn't start eating and Momma refused to care for him, he would be susceptible to a variety of health risks.

When the kids arrived home from school, we checked in on the babies and fed Elmo a small amount from a bottle. I had to ensure he was getting nutrition, but I also held out hope that Lola would come around and start feeding him. I knew the likelihood of that happening was low, but I also knew that God cares deeply for every living being, and the prayers I had whispered throughout the day for this lamb weren't silly or in vain. They were being heard by a powerful, mighty, and relentlessly merciful God.

The next two days were spent racing across town and back home every few hours to bottle-feed Elmo between meetings, site visits, and basketball practice drop-offs. Early Saturday morning, Charlotte and I slipped on winter coats and trekked out for the first feeding of the day. The brothers were snuggled under the heat lamp, and we held our breath as we quietly watched both Tater Tot and Elmo push to their feet, totter over to Momma, and start eating, wildly wagging their little tails with enthusiasm. We couldn't believe our eyes and squeezed each other tightly as we silently cheered on our little Elmo. Standing in the sheep barn with my girl on that cold morning, cheering on a new momma accomplishing a little miracle, felt a lot like standing on holy ground.

A few months later, a friend called asking if we would take in an orphaned calf. Every morning for many months, I would fill a bottle with calf milk replacer, throw on my muck boots, and walk down to the pasture to feed her breakfast. As I walked, I had three dogs running alongside me, two kittens mischievously darting around me, and a dozen sheep running in excitedly from the other field.

One morning, I started to tear up as I held the bottle

and looked the calf, Betsy, in the eye. I may sound crazy, but I saw light where I once saw only fear. I know—she is a cow. But her eyes looked different. In just under a week, she had transformed from a newly orphaned and frightened calf into a beloved member of our herd. As she sucked down her nutrients, I laughed at the sights around me. Ellie the kitten jumped around Teddy the sheep while he tried to sniff her in what can only be described as confusion. Dora the Lab stood stoically at the pasture gate, watching Betsy with intensity. She had been by Betsy's side since day one; I like to imagine she was silently rooting for her.

When our neighbor Mr. Bob gifted us with a llama and an alpaca in need of rescue, we all fell hard for Larry the llama and Alfie the alpaca. I learned everything I could about caring for these gentle creatures. They moved into the pasture alongside our sheep and our miniature donkey, Daddy Donk, settling easily onto our farm. We adored their quirky personalities, and Larry quickly stole my heart. His goofy smile and lopsided gallop toward me whenever I stepped into the pasture could make even the bleakest day bright.

Larry lived with us for just under three years before he suddenly became lethargic. I spent hours in the pasture with him over several days, consoling, singing, and praying over him. He would lay with his head in my lap as I would cry. When he looked up at me, eyes pleading, it left me feeling utterly helpless. I had two different vets out to check him, and he was on a rigorous cocktail of medicine and nutrients. Every two hours, I would administer a shot or vitamins through a syringe. One morning, three days after he had become ill, I woke and immediately looked out the window to check on him. My breath caught in my throat when I saw him lying on his side; I thought we had lost him. At the same moment, Dave ran in and said, "He's still breathing! Go! I'll get the kids to school!"

I threw on boots and ran to the pasture, tears pouring down my cheeks. I brought him medicine and food and bent down to sit beside him. I was able to roll him off his side to administer his medicine. He nibbled a few bites of food out of my hand, which felt hopeful. From that first moment I saw him from the window until the one when he was eating out of my palm, his best pals stood guard over him. Alfie and Daddy Donk never left his side. They knew. The words "steadfast friendship and perseverance" resonated at that moment.

For the better part of the next day, our entire family was in the pasture dispensing medicine, administering shots and electrolytes, hand-feeding, bringing fresh water, shoveling poo, replenishing hay, and moving the sheep to another pasture. It was a long day of good, hard work. There wasn't a single complaint from the kids. We all loved this goofy llama of ours and would do whatever it took to help him fight.

Five days later, after around-the-clock care, Dave and I made the gut-wrenching decision that it was time to let him go. He had declined quickly, and our veterinarians told us the parasite that had now taken up residence in his brain had affected more organs, and he was suffering greatly. We let the kids say goodbye before they left to go to school for the day. My momma's heart ached so deeply watching my babies have to let go of the hope we had all clung to so desperately for our Larry. I couldn't understand why God would allow this beautiful creature to suffer and why He wasn't answering our prayers for healing. I was heartbroken.

Luke was too young for school and stayed with me in the sheep barn while we waited for the vet to arrive. We sat there, Luke in my lap and Larry beside us, his head resting on my leg, talking about heaven and Jesus and how much Larry was going to be missed here on the farm. I stroked Larry's head and spoke words of love over him as he closed his eyes. I turned on the music on my phone as we sat there waiting. The song "Find You Here" started to play. Sitting on the hay, my tears steadily falling on Larry's head, the lyrics, "You can see my pain, and it breaks your heart," felt like a Divine message. It was a gift to listen to the poignant lyrics amid such sorrow. The words served as a reminder that, even though we didn't get our llama miracle, God was right there with us in that little barn. He didn't leave us there alone.

Farm life can be both beautiful and brutal. That day was certainly one of the hardest days. While we've witnessed hundreds of joy-filled miracles here on this little patch of land, we've also experienced deep grief. On that cold and dreary morning, I knew it was okay to sit in the grief while wholly anticipating the joy. My dear friend Andrea, who is acutely familiar with farm life, shared wisdom with me as I grieved. "Being His means holding all of it—the miracles and the pain—and still raising our hands and saying, 'I don't understand this, and I wanted a different ending to this chapter, but I can still trust that you are good.'" I have held this wisdom closely throughout the years: Despite the hard, God is always, only good.

As the years here on our farm have passed, God has often used my sheep to teach me more about His heart for His kids. Poignantly, caring for my flock has brought Psalm 23 to life in meaningful ways.

The Lord is my shepherd;

I shall not want.

He makes me to lie down in green pastures;

He leads me beside the still waters.

He restores my soul;

He leads me in the paths of righteousness

For His name's sake. (Psalm 23: 1-3, NKJV)

A typical morning here on the farm finds me on our front porch, steaming mug in hand, welcoming the new day while watching our animals graze contentedly in the pasture, often lying down in the shade to rest or meandering over to the pond for water.

Yet yesterday morning, I noticed that, because our weather had been unusually hot and dry, our front pasture had lost all of the vibrancy and nutrients from spring and summer. The land was no longer a lush and vibrant green, instead it was a dry and barren brown. As I watched the sheep struggle to find a measly morsel of grass, I knew it was time. We needed to move the animals to another field in order to let their normal pasture rest and recover. In the new field, they would have fresh grass, a new pond, and plenty of shade. We prepared all morning for the move—inspecting and mending fences and moving food troughs and hay bales.

Once the pasture was secure, we brought over Sadie (our horse), Daddy Donk, and Alfie. These three are best buds and walked over together, entering their new pasture with ease and confidence.

The sheep were a different story. Teddy and Earl (our rams) were fairly easy to move. However, Earl kept getting distracted by patches of grass or wildflowers. He tended to wander off the path and wouldn't listen to my gentle nudging ("Focus, Earl. Focus . . ."). Teddy, meanwhile, followed me diligently. He was born to Trixie, several years ago, and as one of Trixie's kids, he trusts me and follows my voice faithfully.

Next up, Snowy and Baa Baa and her kids: Mary, Daisy, Ben, and Nate. Baa Baa was adopted from another farm and when she came to us, she was extremely timid and skittish. As a result of her wariness—despite years of trying to win her over with kindness and an ample supply of treats—her lambs have always been skittish as well. This made moving them to a new pasture extremely difficult. Every time we started to guide the flock toward the new pasture, one would panic and bolt off in the wrong direction and the rest would follow suit.

It took hours of patiently guiding the herd, allowing them to rest when needed, and calmly assuring them of their safety, to finally get them corralled in the sheep barn. Once they were safely tucked inside, we used cattle panels in order to direct the sheep along a walled-off path. But after they made it through, they ran off in the wrong direction and became trapped between a thorny bramble bush and the opposite side of the new pasture fence. Eventually, painstakingly, we guided them to the correct fence and cheered joyfully as they crossed the threshold and we latched the gate behind them.

While moving sheep between pastures is likely a foreign concept to you, dear reader, I have done it enough times to know that, at least for our little hobby farm, this experience is pretty typical.

As I tried desperately to assure these gentle creatures that this move was for their benefit and they had nothing to be afraid of, I was convicted of my own ability to panic and run off course when God is leading me toward something new. Similar to when I was first approached to film a television show—my natural inclination was to say no and stay doing what I was already doing. The new thing being asked of me was scary and it felt safer to avoid this new path rather than to walk down it into the unknown.

I was also reminded of the importance of recounting the stories of God's faithfulness in my life to my kids (like my Trixie and her boy Teddy—he trusts me because his mom knew I was trustworthy). Yes, I pray my children find their own faith, not a copycat version of my own. Yet if the foundation of trustworthiness is built now, it will be much easier for them to seek His voice amidst the chaos of the world later.

Working to guide the skittish sheep, I realized it is certainly no coincidence that the Bible refers to "sheep" no less than 220 times.

W. Phillip Keller, a writer and an actual shepherd by trade, writes in his book *A Shepherd Looks at Psalm 23*:

> There were events which at the time seemed like utter calamities; there were paths down which He led me that appeared like blind alleys; there were days He took me through which were well nigh black as night itself. But all in the end turned out for my benefit and my well-being.
>
> With my limited understanding as a finite human being I could not always comprehend His management executed in infinite wisdom. With my natural tendencies to fear, worry, and ask "why," it was not always simple to assume that He really did know what He was doing with me. There were times I was tempted to panic, to bolt, and to leave His care. *Somehow I had the strange, stupid notion I could survive better on my own.* Most men and women do.

This morning, on the other side of that move, my sheep are in the west-facing pasture, grazing contentedly on the abundant grass. They feared the move, they fought against the move, they seemingly had the "strange, stupid notion" that they could survive better on their own. Yet, as their shepherd, I knew better. I knew there were green pastures awaiting them just on the other side of the struggle. I knew they were headed toward something better than the field with meager offerings where they would've stayed simply because it was known and comfortable. Yes, the path to get there was rocky and scary, but I never left them. I was right there, guiding them, assuring them. When they veered off course, I didn't get angry. I knew they were afraid. I gently, lovingly, patiently reminded them that I was right there. They could trust me. Now and in the future, I would never let them down.

And this morning, I can understand a little better why God often calls us His sheep. And why He can be trusted as my Good Shepherd.

CHAPTER 17

AT LEAST WE DON'T
HAVE AN ELEPHANT

One afternoon, Charlotte and I were out in the pasture cleaning up after her horse, Sadie. We had filled dozens of wheelbarrow loads and deposited them in the garden for fertilizer, yet we had barely made a dent in the immense number of piles left to be cleared. I looked around and felt defeated. We had worked so hard for two full days, and there were still mounds as far as the eye could see.

Charlotte looked right at me, shrugged, and said, "Well, at least we don't have an elephant."

At that moment, though my back ached, my hands were raw, and my toes were freezing, I forgot all about the physical discomfort and clutched my sides, laughing. I realized how, as we get older and hardened by the harshness of this world, we forget that simple, innocent optimism is a gift always at our disposal. Cynicism and bitterness creep in over the years and whisper lies— *You'll never make a difference. The problem is too massive, too complicated, too hard for little ol' you to tackle. Who do you think you are?*

And we stop before we start.

When we first began building and restoring homes two decades ago, we never set out to do so on television. If I had been overwhelmed by the idea of renovating sixteen homes in seven months every year with a camera following along, or if I had believed the work to be impossible or had feared how our lives could change or had been too worried about the keyboard warriors' critiques, I never would have started. I would have stayed in my safe lane and missed out on the sheer delight that comes with following my adventurous, fun-loving, spoiling-His-kids Father.

I wouldn't have been able to work with all of the families that we have, or move our kids to Charleston for six weeks to live beside the ocean while we worked on a competition show called *Rock the Block,* or travel back and forth as a family to tackle a ludicrous dream of reno-vating a Tuscan villa for dear friends. I wouldn't have ever believed that the job I get to do every day could result in work that has changed my life in unbelievable ways. I would never have been able to share about our Berry Farm on a national stage. I would never have been able to share about the beauty of adoption in *People* magazine and on the *Today* show. I would never have been able to live out my childhood dream of authoring a book (now two!). The wildness of it all blows me away when I stop and think about it.

When we first said yes to filming a television show about our life and our work, we mistakenly assumed God would use the show to further our nonprofit work or advocate for adoption. While He has done these things, our thinking was much smaller than what I now believe He had planned. This work of restoring homes, this work that we love, is about so much more. We have been given the immense privilege of sharing with the world the personal stories of the families we work with. We've shared stories of families overcoming illnesses and deployed dads serving our country. We've reno-vated a home as a surprise for a family battling child-hood cancer and have created homes for our own family members, making beautiful memories along the way.

We have become dear friends with many of our clients and have watched as they go on to build lives within the walls we once restored. We have been blessed with friendships that we never would have anticipated— having lived alongside our production crew for six seasons, they've become an extension of our family. We've shared countless meals, birthdays, celebrations, and long days of filming together. I've stayed up until two A.M. with Kim, Melissa, Lindsey, and Sara, staging houses for an early-morning reveal. The owner of our production company has worked beside us and our camera operators in the front yard, hours before the homeowner arrives, laying sod. Every person on our team does everything in their power to ensure the homes are perfect and the shows we create together are entertaining and joyful.

Thinking back to when Dave and I restored our first historic home, I can now see that God was planting the seeds for me to use my creativity and Dave his natural talent as a carpenter. As we built Dave's construction business and moved so often in those early years, I learned how to create a home by living there and understanding how I wanted each space to feel and function. Each house we renovated and moved into was a chance to be creative in a new way.

While being in front of a camera was never on my radar, and my kids have now grown up with this weird, new life as their norm, Dave and I go to work just like every other parent around the world does. We come home from work, we help with homework, we cook dinner, and we say prayers. We cheer on the sidelines of soccer fields and basketball courts. We clean dinner dishes and lament the never-ending piles of laundry. We care for our little menagerie of animals on the farm. We lead a fairly normal, far-from-glamorous life.

My simple prayer at the beginning of this journey continues to be my prayer each and every day: *Let me shine your light, Lord.* Some days, I'm cranky and tired and I don't want a camera filming my every move. On those days, I certainly don't feel like a light. Some days, I'm overwhelmed and stressed by the weight of managing a small business, the thousands of design decisions to be made, or the lack of empty space on our family's calendar. On those days, I certainly don't feel like a light. Some days it's excruciatingly hot and humid and I just want to get my job done without worrying about my frizzy hair, or it's bitterly cold and I want to wear a warm jacket without worrying if it's too scratchy for my microphone. On those days, I certainly don't feel like a light.

Thankfully, God can make up for all of my humanness. Whenever I feel unfit for this job He has called me to, He fills the gap. Whenever I'm fighting physical exhaustion, He fills the gap. For every single lack on my part, He fills every single gap. And, while I don't exactly know *how* to be a light, I do know the One who *is* the light. I trust that He shines through me.

The first time a kind lady walked up to me in the Atlanta airport terminal as I rushed to make a connection and specifically used the word "light" to describe how she felt watching our show, I was taken aback. I hugged her as my arms tingled, covered in goosebumps. I wondered how she had come up with that specific word about a show focused on home renovations. It seemed implausible. Since then, I've been told this by countless people, and each time, it feels like a God-wink reminding me that He is working in and through all of this.

When He commands something like *Shine my light*, even in the entertainment industry—an industry notoriously known for glitz and glamour and shock and drama—He is faithful. When the false headlines, the scathing reviews, or the harsh critics taunt loudly, I can keep my eyes focused on Him and pray the words He taught me to pray once again. *Lord, allow me to shine your light.* I can turn it all over and pray that He uses my doubts, my feelings of ineptitude, my gifts, and my creativity to point others to Him. I can pray that He keeps humility in my heart and helps me to look to Him alone for my worth, not the words of affirmation or judgment from others.

Just like that day in the pasture, I had to learn to simply start with the one pile in front of me—*the sizzle reel*—then move to the next—*the pilot episode*—and then the next—*filming season one*. And then, I moved to the next pile. And little by little, I believe I *have* been able to make a difference.

CHAPTER 18

GO BACK THE WAY YOU CAME

Seven years have now passed since God gave me the vision of a starting line, with our family standing at the threshold of a freshly paved path. Coincidentally, the number seven is biblically significant and served as a symbolic reference in ancient Israelite culture to communicate a sense of "fullness" or "completeness."* Seven years ago, I didn't feel complete or full. At the time, I had no context for what the freshly paved path in my dream symbolized. I was still healing from the trauma and ex-

* Maurice H. Farbridge's book, *Studies in Biblical and Semitic Symbolism*, 134-37.

haustion of the battle to get our daughter home; I was working tirelessly to grow our small business, and our nonprofit work had begun to ebb and flow and change even as it crept in and shaped my identity. I couldn't see how I began to place value in the work, in the *doing* and the striving. It wasn't until the work was stripped away and we were forced to relinquish control that God was able to redeem and heal and lead our family along the new path He had planned for us all along.

Over these past seven years, a lesson from the life of the prophet Elijah in 1 Kings 17 has resonated deeply in my spirit. In this passage, God sets Elijah apart and prepares him privately for his upcoming public ministry. God sent him away to hide by the shores of a quiet stream. There, God fed Elijah each day by sending a raven with food. Did you catch that? A *bird* brought Elijah food. A bird. Elijah was completely reliant on God, and God provided faithfully. Elijah goes on to multiply a widow's food and raise her son from the dead. Through all of this, God was teaching Elijah to trust even when the situation made zero rational sense. Next, Elijah defeated the prophets of Baal through the supernatural and mighty power of the Lord at Mount Carmel (1 Kings 18). God taught that if He commands us to do something, He will provide a way for us to do it.

At the start of 1 Kings 19, just after all these powerful

"mountaintop experiences," rather abruptly and unexpectedly, we find Elijah afraid and running for his life. In the desert, under the shade of a solitary broom tree, Elijah, in his desperation, cried out, "I've had enough, Lord."

Even when Elijah appeared to have turned away from God's call on his life, God never turned away or gave up on Elijah. Instead, God tenderly cared for Elijah's physical needs, preparing him for the journey ahead. He fed Elijah two small meals of bread and water, and those meals were stretched to sustain Elijah for the next forty days. After Elijah was nourished, he heard God speak. Twice, God asked, "What are you doing here, Elijah?" He called Elijah by name. How gentle and personal of our Father. Then, instead of taking away the immediate threat from which Elijah originally ran, He said, "Go back the way you came. . . ." (1 Kings 19:15) He sent him back. God didn't remove the hard thing, yet He sustained Elijah through the journey.

I am ridiculously grateful for the fact that these stories are recorded in the Bible to give me examples of the heroes of my faith, wavering and afraid. It makes me feel less crazy when I find myself in a similar situation. I've seen how so often God works in my heart in the quiet, hidden moments. I believe God was preparing my heart in the years leading up to that "starting line" vision for what was to come with this much more public life I now lead. Elijah's story also reminds me how trustworthy and merciful my God is—no matter the situation. He gently whispers, *I am right here. I won't leave. You can go back and do this with a fresh heart. You can trust me.*

I know that over the past seven years, I have been in Elijah's shoes. I have found myself wanting to crawl under the shade of a solitary tree and hide out for a bit. I have told God that I don't want to be out in front. I have witnessed miracles and experienced the abundance of God's mercy, yet the enemy's lies and accusations can still drive me straight into the murky pit of despair. How could little ol' me get on a stage and talk about design when I just taught myself as I went, messing up along the way and often feeling like a fraud because I never sought any of this out? I love my work, but I certainly don't feel like an expert. I feel like a mom who wants more time with her kids, a wife who wants a quiet date night with her husband, or an insecure girl who cringes every time the taunts loudly jump off a screen.

Then, when I turn my eyes back to my Mighty God, when I step away from the hustle of this world and quiet my heart and my racing mind, when I open His Word and speak His truth, I feel His power and His refreshing and restoring spirit. When I take the time to slow down and be still, I am sustained once again for the work ahead, no matter how overwhelming it may seem. I can call out the lies of the enemy and step into the truth of who I am. I am a daughter, a beloved child of the King who whispers, *"Jenny, go back the way you came. I'm right here."*

Seven years ago, I didn't know that we would grow from a family of six to a family of seven. I also wasn't sure if our small blueberry farm would make any difference in the world. I didn't know that it would positively impact families in our community and provide a pathway to education for vulnerable teenagers in Zimbabwe. And, most surprisingly, at the time God gave me the vision, I had no way of knowing that we were about to go from building and restoring homes quietly in our town to doing so with cameras following along. Since then, we were somehow graciously accepted into the living rooms of millions of people around the world (a fact I truly can't wrap my mind around), and consequently our day-to-day lives have changed significantly. We just kept stepping forward in faith, trusting God and loving the people He places in our path.

I'm struck by the way God works in the lives of ordinary people, in ways we may not understand or comprehend at the time, that potentially have ripple effects for generations to come. Oh, how I pray my kiddos will learn to trust God and follow His lead even when it makes no sense, and I pray that they will learn the joy of living with open hands because of Dave's and my example. I pray our work in business and at our farm will teach them to live generously with their time, talents, and resources. I pray our global friendships will teach them that no matter where we live, what we look like, or what language we speak, we are all created in God's image, and we are all of indescribable worth. I pray they will learn to love those around them, near and far, in deep and tangible ways.

And, dear reader, my prayer for us both is that we would remain steadfast in our faith by remembering God's faithfulness in our past. And, in our remembering, may we learn to confidently trust Him with our steps and be fueled to love those around us well. I believe we all have great adventures in store and that we are all here—living and breathing, right now, this very day, at this exact point in history—for a purpose. The story isn't over yet.

ACKNOWLEDGMENTS

This book was simply a wild idea and a hodgepodge of stories before the wise counsel and guidance of my gifted editor, Katy Hamilton. Without her, as well as my dear friend and literary agent, Stephen Morrison, I couldn't have pieced together this puzzle. I'm forever indebted to you both for your belief in this project and for your steadfast encouragement.

While it feels surreal to say "my publishing team," I can't imagine working with a better group of people than those at Convergent, under the leadership of Tina Constable, Theresa Zoro, and Derek Reed. I sincerely appreciate the contributions of Steven Boriack, Campbell Wharton, Gail Gonzalez, Rachel Tockstein, Alisse Goldsmith-Wissman, and Jessalyn Foggy.

Thank you also to Joe Perez, Ashley Shoemaker, Loren Noveck, and Liz Carbonell. And to the collaborative efforts of Jessie Bright and Buddy Whitlock: Thank you for using your artistic gifts in order to create a beautiful cover design. To Bethany Carroz, I echo what my friend said when she saw your watercolor painting for the cover: *"It's perfect. That is Jenny Marrs."* You captured my heart and our family in your art and I'll treasure this painting always. And a big thank-you to Susanna Lea and Brian Samuels for always being in my corner.

To RIVR Media and our production team, thank you for the laughter, love, and hard work you've all poured into *Fixer to Fabulous* over the years: Lori Stryer, Stephanie Ellis, Angie Jedlicka, Bryan Stratte, Elise Sabbeth, Jerome Jarnigan, Jason Bernardi, David Bollinger, Holly Markle, Andrew Jedlicka, Adam Neil, Grant Johnson, Sam McDonald, Mike D'Avello, Tanja Heffner, Sara Donahue, Tyler Whitlock, and my right-hand girls, Lindsey Lustrino and Kim Brown. I am forever grateful to be surrounded by the best team daily. Many thanks to Matt Treweiler, Bridget Cleary, and Loren Ruch for your unwavering support of our work. I appreciate you all immensely.

To my tribe: You have prayed for and celebrated this project from the beginning, and I'm grateful for the privilege of walking through life alongside each of you: Brandy Becker, George Corton, Chanika Ogle, Melissa Halford, Corrie Rusch, Kristin Buse, Carrie Balthazar, Brynn D'Avello, Andrea Young, Rebecca Dunmire, Ricky and Tracie Draehn, Kim Brown, Lindsey Lustrino, Allie Wells, Beth Waldmann, Brianna Wells, Lauri Meidell, Lindsay Peattie, Molly Bottoms, and Vicki Calonge. One million hugs and thanks to Jennifer Armbruster, Cassidy McCalla, and Paige Martin for reading early versions of the manuscript and providing thoughtful feedback and ongoing prayers.

To those who attended that very first birthday party on Beechwood Drive, shortly after we moved to town—Katrin Clubine, Casey Rivard, and Debbie McElroy—you made this place feel like home. And to Cathy Zenker, Muffy Heman, Kristin Aschoff, Lisa Crossett, and Annie Gray, whom I met in my earliest days in Arkansas, I am so grateful for your friendship.

Before I penned the first words, I asked my collegiate house mom, Mama Tay, to pray for this book. She was my cheerleader earthside, and, gracious, I miss her, but I know her prayers cover these pages, and I am immensely grateful for the fact that she "enjoyed talking to Him" about me.

To the one who stood in the gap and loved my girl for me when we were physically separated by an ocean: Dr. Laure. How can I ever thank you enough for all that you did for our family? My gratitude to you extends into Eternity. And to Tresor, thank you for continuing to care for the kids we love in your community. You are doing the hard work every day and it has been an honor and a privilege to stand alongside you all of these years. To Pastor John and Orpah, I can't recall ever meeting a more God-fearing, joyful-despite-circumstances, and humble husband and wife team. You are truly living in the center of God's will and call on your lives and it is the joy of my life to call you friends and co-laborers. Thank you for inspiring me to live and love well.

My parents, Joan and Steve, fielded countless questions and reminded me of fuzzy details from my childhood. Most of all, they've taught me to be brave by trusting in God's faithfulness throughout my life. They, along with my sisters, Angie and Lori, and my brother, Steven, prayed for this book and cheered me on even when the blank screen taunted me (along with Rob, Bryan, and Christina, of course).

Dave's family—Donna, David, Bridget, Matt, Karey, and

Katie—immediately welcomed me into their fold. Words can hardly convey my gratitude for the love they have shown me over the years. From the moment I moved to Arkansas, they embraced me and made me feel at home here.

These pages contain my five miracle stories: Ben, Nathan, Sylvie, Charlotte, and Luke. I wanted all of you to have a record of how faithful God has been to our family. I've said it before, and I'll say it again: Each of you makes this world a brighter place, and the privilege of being your momma is the greatest joy of my life.

To Dave: This story isn't just my story. It's *our* story. It's the story of fighting fear and holding on to Hope, *together*. It's the story of two dreamers who built a life together. It's the story of learning in the dark what can only be understood in the light. Words are insufficient to thank you for being by my side on this wild ride called life. I couldn't ask for a better friend, father to our children, or once-in-a-lifetime great love. Thank you for being you.

A GUIDED JOURNAL PRACTICE

I strongly believe in the practice of intentionally remembering God's faithfulness in my life. As I wrote this book, I often referred back to the journals I have kept over the years, and even used some journal snippets within the chapters. It's a practice that has sustained me, and always reminds me of one of my favorite verses from Deuteronomy:

> But don't be afraid *of them! Just* remember *what the Lord your God did to Pharaoh and to all the land of Egypt.* Remember *the great terrors the Lord your God sent against them. You saw it all with your own eyes! And* remember *the miraculous signs and wonders, and the strong hand*

and powerful arm with which he brought you out of Egypt. (Deuteronomy 7:18-19, NLT, emphasis added)

Moses offers an antidote for fear: remembering. Three times in this passage, he instructs the Israelites to fight fear, to stand against anxiety, and to remain steadfast in their faith by remembering God's faithfulness in their past. Although I find myself in different circumstances than the context of this passage, I too can resist fear by looking back at God's faithfulness in my life and remembering.

Even still, in the busyness of my days, I often get distracted by my to-do list or the seemingly endless cycle of doom-and-gloom news reports, and neglect taking the time to *remember*. Which is why, on the first morning of every new year, I can be found seated in front of a roaring fire with a steaming mug in hand and my worn hardback journal in my lap. I spend the early-morning hours recording the big adventures, the little milestones, and the mundane moments from the previous year. *I intentionally set aside time to remember.* After writing out God's faithfulness over the past twelve months, I pray over the pages in gratitude. I figuratively lay those pages at His feet as a gift of praise.

After I have remembered, I look ahead. Specifically, I record prayers for the coming year. I prefer this over forming New Year's resolutions, which are based on my own willpower and grit. I've found that as I pray the prayers throughout the next year, they redirect my heart, attitude, and actions to the One who authors my story in ways I could never begin to hope or imagine on my own.

If you've been curious about how to incorporate a journaling practice into your spiritual life, perhaps this can serve as your invitation to start. There isn't a blueprint for this tradition but I tend to follow a similar process each year. I begin with a prayer of gratitude and then I spend multiple pages jotting prayers that are specific and personal to each member of my family. Next, I list out prayers for our family as a whole, our extended family and friends, our business, or anything pressing in that particular season. Lastly, I write prayers for myself. I ask God for big and small things. I believe He cares for every detail of my life and no request is insignificant.

This yearly check-in is a vital spiritual practice for me, yet it's not a standalone ritual. I continue to pray through these prayers during the year. I read through the pages often and jot notes in the margins where prayers have been answered or have changed. I also continue to journal throughout the year. Journaling is how I process the world around me and name the ways God is actively working in my life. Oftentimes, I'll open my worn journals and find myself penning thoughts that I didn't even realize were lingering subconsciously until they surfaced through the written word.

These pages are essentially letters to my Heavenly Father and have taken various forms over the years. Sometimes they're bulleted lists, other times scribbled half-sentences, and, most often, ineloquent thoughts. I simply write and pray. Below I've pulled a few examples from my journals to serve as a reference.

On the first day of this past year, I began my pages with these words of gratitude:

Heavenly Father, thank you for an abundant and incredible year. Your faithfulness, mercy, kindness, protection, and guidance are a trustworthy anchor in my life. I am so grateful for our health and for your protection as we worked and traveled this past year. Thank you for the

*words you gave me and the way you helped and guided
me as I wrote this new book. Thank you for the farm, the
kids' teachers, their sports teams and friends, and our beloved animals. Thank you for the adventures and travels
we experienced as a family.*

Then, I went on to thank God for specifics for each person
in our family, such as the way Dave leads us with integrity and
strength, and Ben's kind and gentle heart. I thanked Him for
Nathan's gift of leadership and the way he loves big, and for
Sylvie's generosity and boldness for Jesus. I expressed gratitude for Charlotte's compassion and deep love for God, and
for the laughter and joy Luke brings to our family.

Over the years, my prayers for the kids have changed de-
pending on the circumstances for that year. I pray specifics
over each child and also for them as siblings and for us as their
parents. An example of one of these prayers from 2022:

*Be a wide river of protection (Isaiah 33:21) around our
home and our family. Make our home a shelter of grace,
safety, love, and peace. Protect us physically—keep us
healthy. Protect us spiritually—keep us safe from the evil
one. Be our shield against his fiery arrows. Protect us
relationally—keep our marriage strong, keep our connections to the kids strong. Keep the kids safe online. Protect
their eyes and hearts and minds. Be on guard and alert us
if something is amiss. Give us wisdom as we parent in
this new season of life with preteens. Give us discernment,
gentleness, and patience. Allow the kids to flourish at
school. Surround them with good friends. Strengthen
their walk with you. Help Dave and me to point them to
you and build a strong foundation of security and love to*

carry them throughout their lives. May they shine your light brightly in this world.

For our work with *Fixer to Fabulous*, I've recorded a similar prayer many years in a row. Specifically, in 2021, I wrote:

Bring the right people on to our team. Allow us to create a show that points people to you. May you receive all the glory. Draw others in because they see a light in us that points to you. Protect our hearts from pride. Give us strength, energy, patience, and creativity. Help us not to be overwhelmed by the fear or the pressure to please man. Keep humility in our hearts. Help us to look to you for our worth, not the words or affirmation or judgment of others. Thank you for the opportunities before us this year, may we steward our gifts well.

At the outset of writing this book, in 2023, I wrote:

Please give me the words for this book, Lord. I cannot do this in my own strength or ability. Provide me with discernment to know what to write about—which stories do you want me to share? I want to be a light pointing others to you. Give me the words, and supernatural time, creativity, and energy to write it.

Now, two years later, holding the nearly finished manuscript in my hands, I can look back and see how God so clearly answered my simple prayer in 2023. And looking back over the decade of recording these prayers, I remain immensely grateful for His steadfast faithfulness.

I've included prompts below to guide your practice. There's no need to wait for the first day of a new year; it's always a good time to reflect on the events of the past twelve months and pray for what's ahead. Feel free to jot memories and prayers in the space below each prompt. Most important, know that there is not a right or wrong way to do this. There is not a formula for the number of requests or a specific order in which to list your prayers. Simply take a deep breath and ask God to align your heart and your prayers with His, and begin.

Remember Prompts

1. Create a column of the past twelve months (see facing page). Beside each month, start listing everything you can remember happening during that time. (Tip: I often look at photos on my phone to kick-start my memory.) This can be a quick bulleted list, the point is to remember what happened, and we'll reflect on it next.

2. Read through your list and ask God to show you how He was working in these situations. Jot down anything that comes to mind as you do so.

....

....

....

....

....

JANUARY	
FEBRUARY	
MARCH	
APRIL	
MAY	
JUNE	
JULY	
AUGUST	
SEPTEMBER	
OCTOBER	
NOVEMBER	
DECEMBER	

3. Read through your list again, slowly. As you read, say aloud, "Thank you, Lord, for . . ." and redirect each of these memories to serve as grateful praise.

....

....

....

....

....

Prayer Prompts

1. Write out the names of each person in your family. Underneath each name, write the attributes of their personality that you are most grateful for. Next, write out the ways you have seen God at work in their life this past year. Lastly, in what areas do you pray for God to work in their lives this coming year?

....

....

....

....

....

2. Think through the situations that keep you up at night. Write them down and turn them over to God. Ask Him to work them out for your good and His glory.

....

....

....

....

....

3. What are your hopes for the coming year? Is there some-
    thing unsettled in your spirit? Are you afraid to voice
    hope over a situation? Write it out. And then, turn it over
    to God. Trust Him with your fears and your vulnerable
    confessions.

....

....

....

....

....

4. Consider praying a verse over the year for your family.
    Ask God to lead you to a verse, and when He does, write
    it down. (This doesn't happen instantly, but I always feel
    a calmness in my spirit when I read the verse God leads
    me to for the year and I just know: This is it. You will too.)
    Jot the passage on notecards and place them around
    your home. Pray the verse daily.

....

....

....

....

....

DISCUSSION GUIDE

1. Jenny shares her family's tradition of collecting stones when they travel or have meaningful experiences to serve as a reminder of God's faithfulness. Why is "remembering" an important practice? How do you mark important moments in your life?

2. Reflect upon a time when you were given a glimpse of God at work in your life. What were the circumstances and how did you encounter God?

3. On page xvii, Jenny shares how she has come to live her life by the phrase: "Trust God, love people." How are the

two interconnected? If your life was guided by a phrase, what would it be, or what might you want it to be?

4. Is there something in your life that is waiting for you to take the first step? How can you be encouraged by Zechariah 4:10 ("Do not despise these small beginnings, for the Lord rejoices to see the work begin . . . ," NLT) to take that step?

5. Can you share a time in your life when the path ahead of you seemed unclear, or even blocked, and yet you walked forward in faith? What happened?

6. Jenny talks about how hard it was to move to a new town and the time it took to start feeling like home. What place feels most like home to you? Why?

7. Walking through a season of change is challenging, but in chapter two, Jenny learns an important lesson about God's faithfulness and the sovereignty of His plans. Reflect upon a season of change in your life. What did you learn about yourself during that time? What did you learn about God in that season?

8. As Jenny is going through a difficult period of trying to start a family with Dave, she is bolstered by remembering that "Together, we can do hard things." Name the person (or people) you can lean on when your life takes an unexpected or difficult turn.

9. After years of painful waiting, Jenny and Dave are blessed with twin boys, a gift she views as a reminder of God's abundant blessings. In what ways have you seen God's blessings as abundant in your life?

10. Trusting God doesn't mean that we don't still have fear,

worry, or anxiety. How can we walk in faith even when experiencing fear?

11. The importance of prayer soaks through every story in this book. What role does prayer play in your life?

12. When Jenny and Dave have to leave after visiting Sylvie in the Democratic Republic of the Congo, Jenny says, "I took a deep breath and resolved once again to hand over control to His capable hands." In what area of your life right now might you need to hand over control to God?

13. Jenny calls the long, uncertain season of waiting for her daughter to come home the *in-between place*. If you are in the midst of your own in-between season, how are you feeling? If you're on the other side of the wait, do you have any encouragement you can share with others?

14. If adoption is part of your story—as either an adoptive parent or an adopted child—what comes to mind when reading about Jenny's journey to bring Sylvie home to join their family?

15. On page 98, Jenny writes about how, in Deuteronomy, the Israelites were called to write God's commands on the entryways of their homes to serve as a reminder of God's law as the foundation of their household and family. Now Jenny and Dave make it a tradition to write Bible verses in permanent marker directly on the door trim in houses they renovate. Where could you write God's Word to serve as a reminder over your life?

16. Even in the storm, "God's promises remained steadfast," Jenny writes on page 115. What storms have you weathered, and how did you witness God working in that time?

17. In seasons of uncertainty, Jenny knows that she "simply needed to do the one thing right in front of [her], take the one step forward in faith." It sounds easy to take just one step, but why is it hard to do that one thing in front of us?

18. Travel plays an important role in Jenny's life. What has traveling to new places taught you?

19. During a time of exhaustion and uncertainty, Jenny is encouraged by a verse in Judges: "Go with the strength you have . . ." (Judges 6:14, NLT). Where do you need to trust that God's strength is sufficient in your life?

20. Jenny's experience with the animals, especially the sheep, on her farm has given her a new appreciation for how she understands God as a "Good Shepherd." Does seeing God in this way change how you relate to Him?

21. Using the examples of Gideon, Hannah, and Elijah, among others, Jenny shares that she is encouraged by the way God uses flawed humans to carry out his plans. Whose story in the Bible encourages you in your faith?

22. On pages 183–84, Jenny shares the prayers she has for her children, knowing they are watching her story unfold. If you have children, what are your prayers for them as they grow?

23. One of Jenny's prayers is: "I pray they will learn to love those around them, near and far, in deep and tangible ways." What does loving others in this way look like in your life?

24. What adventure is God calling you to next? How can you take the first step forward in faith?

ABOUT THE AUTHOR

JENNY MARRS is a designer, author, and passionate advocate for community transformation, family preservation, and orphan care around the globe. She is the author of *House + Home = Love,* and co-hosts *Fixer to Fabulous* with her husband, Dave. She and Dave live on a small farm in Bentonville, Arkansas, with their five kids and too many animals to count.

Instagram: @jennymarrs
Facebook: jenny.marrs
jennymarrs.com

Also available
from Jenny Marrs

House + Love = Home
Creating Warm, Intentional Spaces for a Beautiful Life

Jenny Marrs
WITH SPECIAL APPEARANCES BY Dave Marrs
CO-HOSTS OF *Fixer to Fabulous*

AVAILABLE WHEREVER BOOKS ARE SOLD